STORIES OF THE MAYAN GODS FROM
BEFORE THE ADVENT OF HUMANS

POPOL VUH

BY STEVEN SELBY

LIMITED FIRST EDITION

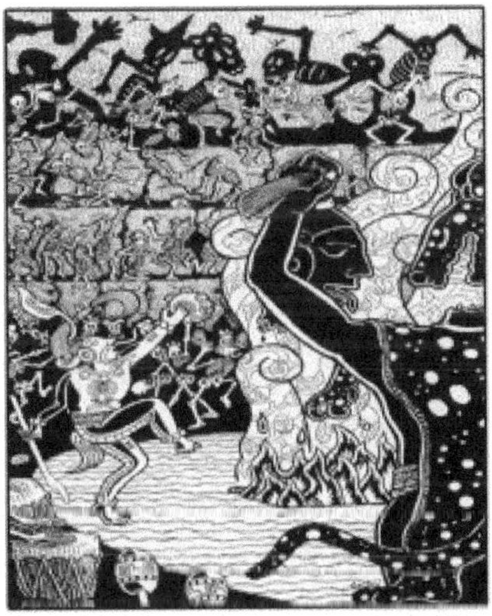

THE POPOL VHU

First edition. March 27, 2024.

Copyright © 2024 Steven Selby.

ISBN: 979-8224139453

Written by Steven Selby.

Also by Steven Selby

Money, Money, Money, The 1%
The Popol Vhu

Table of Contents

INTRODUCTION

Currently, it is believed that the roots of the Maya civilization came from the Olmecs which flourished on the coastal plains of Veracruz and Tabasco which are now part of Mexico as early as 1200 BC. By 100 BC the Izapan culture which developed along the Western and Southern borders of what would become the area of the Mayan civilization had an iconographic form of pictorial writing on stone structures that is very similar to what archaeologists designate as Early Classic Maya AD 300 to 900. These carved hieroglyphic texts were extensively used by the Maya in the form of tall rectangular blocks of stone called stelae. During this period the Maya developed this writing in the form of reliefs carved in stone and plaster and painted to decorate and inscribe their monuments. They also developed a painted form of hieroglyphic text for pottery and inked long lengths of paper which they folded to form books.

By the Post Classic Period AD 1200 carved stone inscriptions were no longer a feature of monuments or buildings but, hieroglyphic text and painting on plaster became the key form of decoration. At the same time, beautiful forms of pottery were made and painted while books of painted images and hieroglyphic writing were abundantly produced. This is especially evident along the East coast of the Yucatan down to central Belize. The writing of Post Classic Maya AD 900 to 1400 includes the increased use of phonetic signs including symbols invented by the Maya.

When the Spanish defeated the Aztecs in AD 1600 it became the responsibility of the Jesuits to control and enlighten the population. How this was accomplished is not in the scope of this book but some aspects are of interest in the writing of the Popol Vuh The Spanish Priesthood adopted young boys of the Mayan ruling class to train them in the ways of the Priesthood and to create leaders they could control. Part of this training was the use of the Roman Alphabet and phonetic sounds in writing. What was accomplished was a way the Maya could write phonetically their languages using the Roman Alphabet. This has centuries later helped in understanding Maya languages and to some extent their original hieroglyphic scripts. The Popol Vuh has been important in this respect.

During the transition and building of "New Spain," there was excessive disruption and pain. The Priesthood was only able to see evil in the old ways of Mayan life while the European religious images were thought to contain supreme good and nothing else was given a chance. To completely eradicate Mayan ideology, books were burned throughout the region of the Mayan Civilization. The European invasion of the Mayan world began in the sixteenth century and by the end of the seventeenth century hundreds of hieroglyphic books had been destroyed but in the early eighteenth century in what is now Guatemala these books still existed. Just as the Mayan people learned to use Christian symbolism to mask their gods, they used the Roman alphabet to mask their ancient texts. Their most notable works, created as alphabetic substitutes for their hieroglyphic books, are the Chilam Balam or "Jaguar Translator" books from the Yucatan and the Popol Vuh from the Guatemala highlands.

Only four hieroglyphic books called "codices" have survived. These four Codices provide our only peek at what these hieroglyphic books may have contained. There is also one Spanish book from this period that describes what little we know of the ways of Indian life at the time of the Spanish conquest. Strangely, it was written by the very person who called for the destruction of all Mayan history, Bishop Landa. What is understandable from the codices is foremost that the Maya were great watchers of the heavens. They knew the movements of the planets and the earth better than European watchers. They devised three calendars that allowed them to see far into the past as well as the future and organized daily time differently. The Popol Vuh suggests that these books or codices would allow readers to be able to see what had been and what would occur.

The authors of the alphabetic Popol Vuh did not include their names but are thought to have been leaders of the Quiche Kingdom during the middle of the sixteenth century. Before 1703 a copy of this alphabetical Popol Vuh found its way to the town of Chuwi La or "Nettles Heights" otherwise known as Chichicastenango. Friar Francisco Ximenes the parish priest during this time made a copy of this alphabetic Popol Vuh and added a Spanish translation alongside the Quichiquil text. In 1830 reforms forced the closing of all monasteries in Guatemala and Friar Ximenes's manuscript was acquired by the library of the University of San Carlos in Guatemala City. In 1854 Etienne Brasseur de Bourbourg, a French priest, took the manuscript to French where it was published in 1861. Since 1911 it has been in the Newberry Library in the US as part of a collection of North American Indian and Mesoamerican manuscripts.

The writers of the alphabetic version of the Popol Vuh tell us that the Quiche rulers once had an ilb'al, a "seeing instrument" or "place to see", where they could know distant events. This instrument was not a crystal ball or a telescope, but a book. This helps explain why the hieroglyphic version was the most precious possession of Quiche rulers. In this book or more likely series of books they could see if war would occur, if there would be death, or if there would be famine, or whether there would be quarrels. They knew it for certain, they could see it. If the hieroglyphic Popol Vuh was anything like the surviving codices it contained systematic accounts of cycles in astronomical and earthly events that served as a complex navigational system for those who wished to see or move beyond the present. If a divinatory reading or pondering was a way of recovering the depth of vision of earlier men then it may have been possible in a "long performance" which covers every major subject in the books to recover a full cosmic sweep of human vision and understanding.

The authors of the phonetic Popol Vuh must have been under extreme pressure with the priesthood actively destroying all traditional Mayan documents while insisting that apprentices learn to write in a way that the clergy could read. The prospect of destroying their most precious books may have forced them to create a parody of what they wanted to protect. This is apparent in the Chilam Balam where much of the writing is so obscure that it is impossible to understand. But, the authors of the phonetic Popol Vuh succeeded in creating a most intriguing set of stories. Bits of which are graphically depicted as far back as early classic stone carvings. From the post-classic period, there are many of these stories depicted on painted walls and pottery and to some extent in the surviving codices. It is also believed that this Popol Vuh may not be complete because other scenes on pottery include the "hero twins" that are not described here.

My first reading of the Popol Vuh left me confused and I remember thinking, "Now what was that all about". I supposed that my confusion was because the origin of these stories was a thousand years before Christ. They were carved in stone during the next thousand years and became a best-selling theme for painted walls, pottery, and books over the next four hundred years. They then were translated from many little-known Mayan languages using a language and writing system that had been forced on them by Spanish strangers and then this manuscript was lost. Then found by chance by a small group of academics and translated again into modern languages—a rather remarkable story in itself. I think they may have made the stories purposely confusing to protect themselves from the eyes of an oppressive priesthood. My rearrangement then is only an attempt at clarification.

What I have tried to do in this book is to make these stories flow in a sequence that is easier to follow. I have since learned that sequential time is all but lost in the Popol Vuh because the stories plot the astronomical movement of Venus, the Moon, the Sun, and Mars, as well as, various constellations including extensive symbolism involving the Milky Way, so say academics who are trying to figure out the complexities of Maya cosmology. In truth, these stories may well be gems in the tapestry of an astrological genius of a lost civilization. The complicated connection of these stories to astronomical events I have only lightly touched upon primarily because this alphabetical Popol Vuh does not elaborate on these details.

In a further attempt to clarify the stories, I have included many illustrations. Other Popol Vuh books generally include redrawn images from artifacts which, while interesting, often fail to illuminate the text. The style I have followed is one where the characters relate to Maya forms while staged in the backgrounds of my creation. In this work, there are over fifty illustrations with the cover as the centerpiece depicting the "Water Lily Jaguar of the Underworld".

Large portions of these stories accrue in a strange underworld called Xibalba. There are many interpretations of this place from the macban to the comical. I have tried to follow the original storyline while illustrating these scenes in an acceptable way for children. It is my recommendation that parents make their own decisions about appropriate context.

A better understanding of the characters, terms, and places in the stories can be found in the Glossary. In Guatemala alone, there are over twenty Mayan dialects, so names often vary from source to source. Generally, pronunciation should follow Spanish forms but with an accent on the last syllable.

I find it astonishing that so few people know the stories of the Popol Vuh. I suppose it is a classic, waiting to be appreciated. I hope that this book can pave the way. ENJOY!

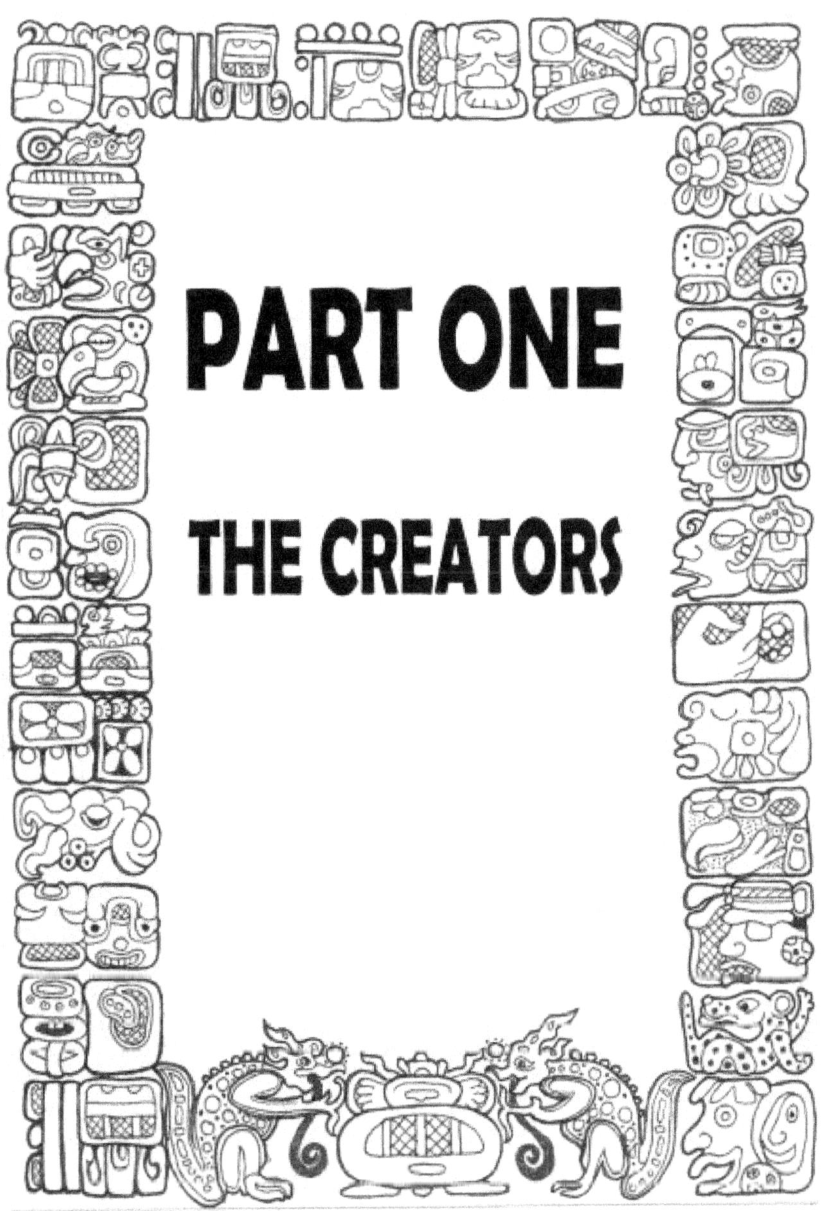

PART ONE

THE CREATORS

PART ONE

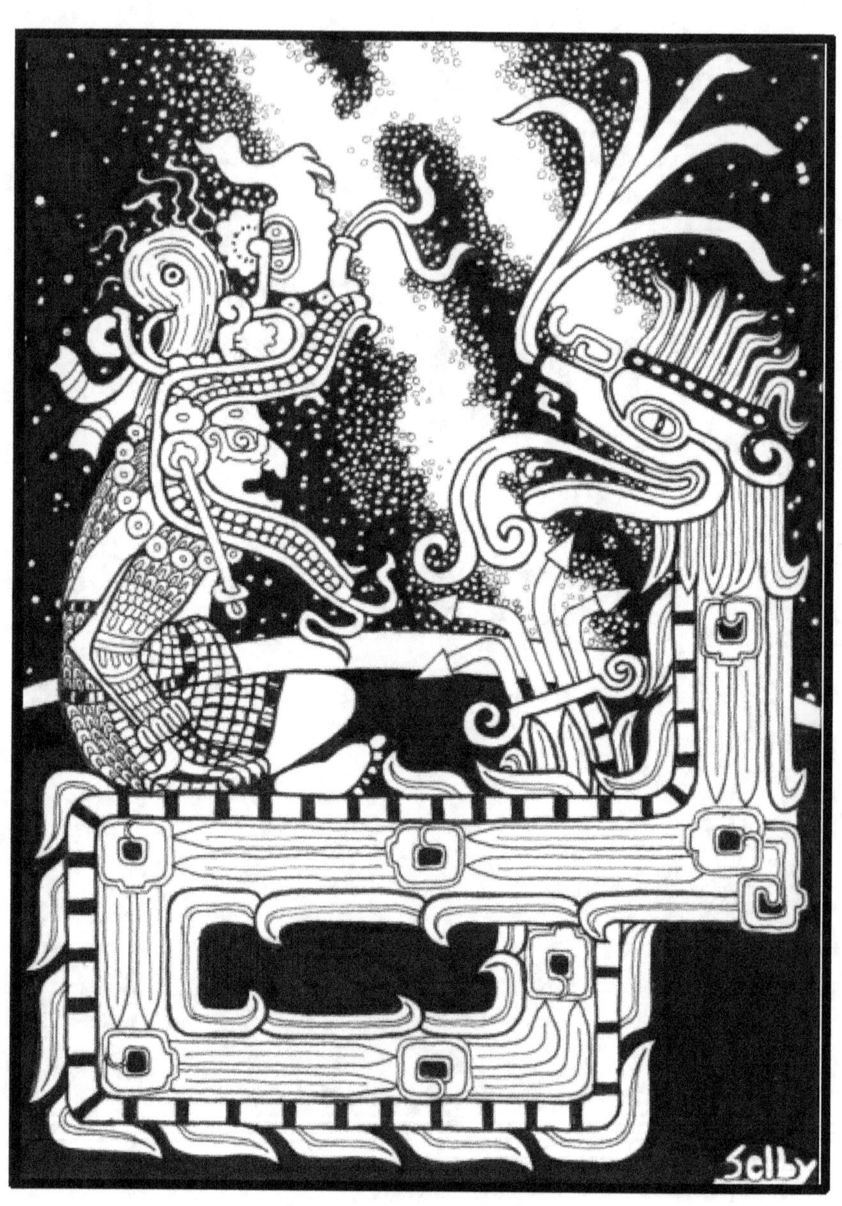

THE CREATORS

THE CREATORS

In the beginning, there was only the sea and the sky. There was no sun, no moon, no stars, just the movement and murmur of the sea. There were no mountains, no canyons, no meadows, no forests, no rocks, no rivers, no fish, no trees, no birds, no insects, no animals, and no people.

But, there was a glimmering light in the endless sea. This was the Maker, Modeler. The Bearer, Begetter. The Creator who will one day be known as the Sovereign Plumed Serpent enclosed in blue-green Quetzal feathers whose knowledge, thinking, and powers are as great as his very being. He is the Heart of Earth and the sovereign God of this world.

Then, in the darkness came the Heart of Sky named Hurakan who is the god of the universe. He came here to the earth in the blackness of the early dawning. He spoke with Sovereign Plumed Serpent, they talked, they thought, they worried and they agreed with each other.

Heart of Earth and Heart of Sky joined their words and their thoughts and conceived the generation and growth of the land, the trees, of animals, and all the creatures of Life. Together they said, "Let it be this way, we will make a platform, a kind of plate and then we will shape it with high and low parts that will be known as mountains and valleys, then we will add water in the form of rivers and lakes. It will be beautiful and then we will fill it with life".

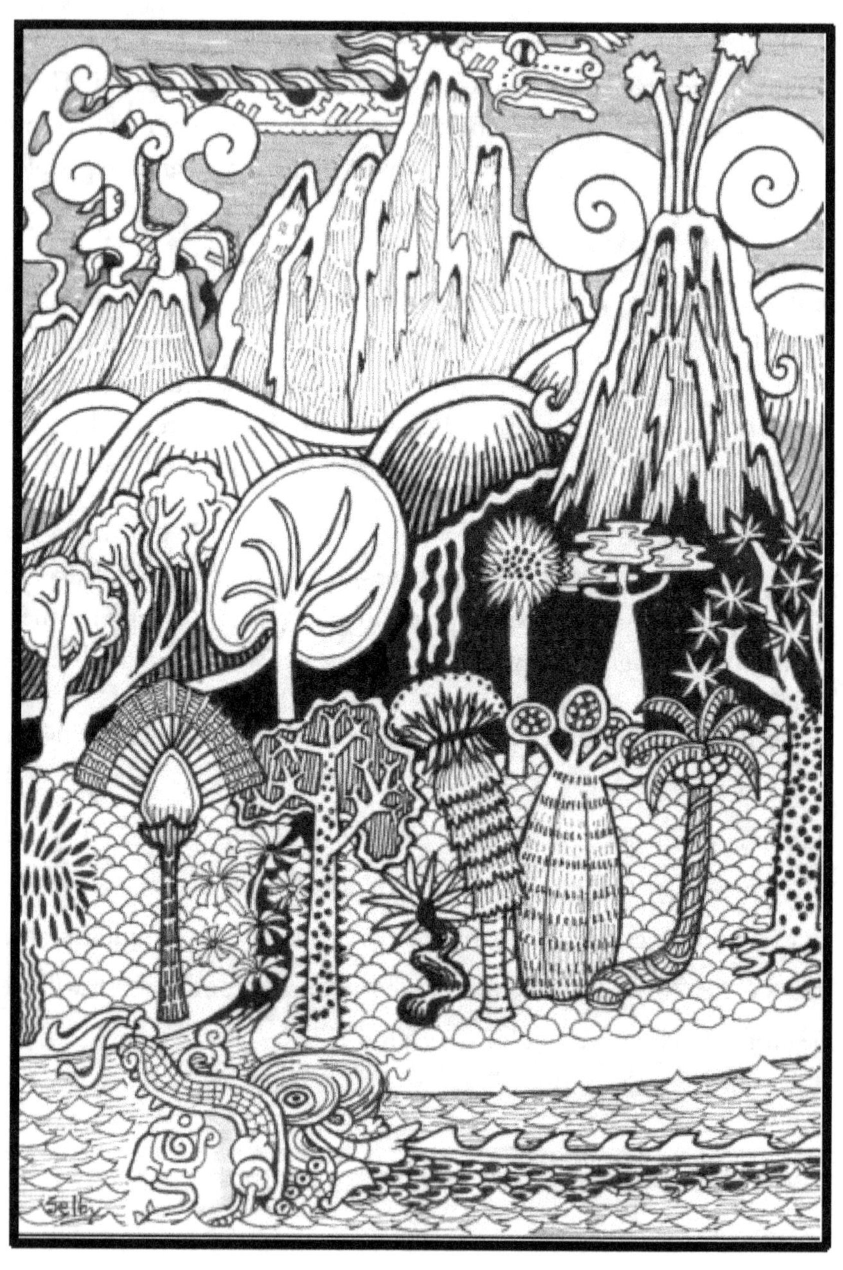

THE DAWNING OF LIFE

It was simply their combined thoughts, their vision, and their combined words that brought forth the land. They said, "Earth." and it came forth like a cloud or mist, rolling back the sea while the mountains arose from the water with their conception of high peaks with valleys between. Some of these peaks sprang forth with plums of smoke and fire. Lowlands, marshes, and deserts began to appear as the sea moved away.

They then thought of how the rivers should be. Some they placed in canyons while others splashed and crashed among rocks. Others shot off great cliffs forming clouds of mist and spray while others collected in slow-moving masses of water moving in wavy lines toward the sea. They even placed rivers below the earth and made caves and cenotes just for their beauty.

When they were pleased with this formation of a platform they began the creation of the plants. First, they put the grasses in the fields, rushes in the quiet waters, and mosses on wet rocks but the land was great so they created trees.

They could see how all of this must work together so they began creating plants for food. Fruit trees, nut trees, banana trees, berry bushes. Plants big and small would feed all of the animals and insects that they wanted to make, and to make it all pleasing, they added leaves that changed colors and flowers of endless designs and bright colors.

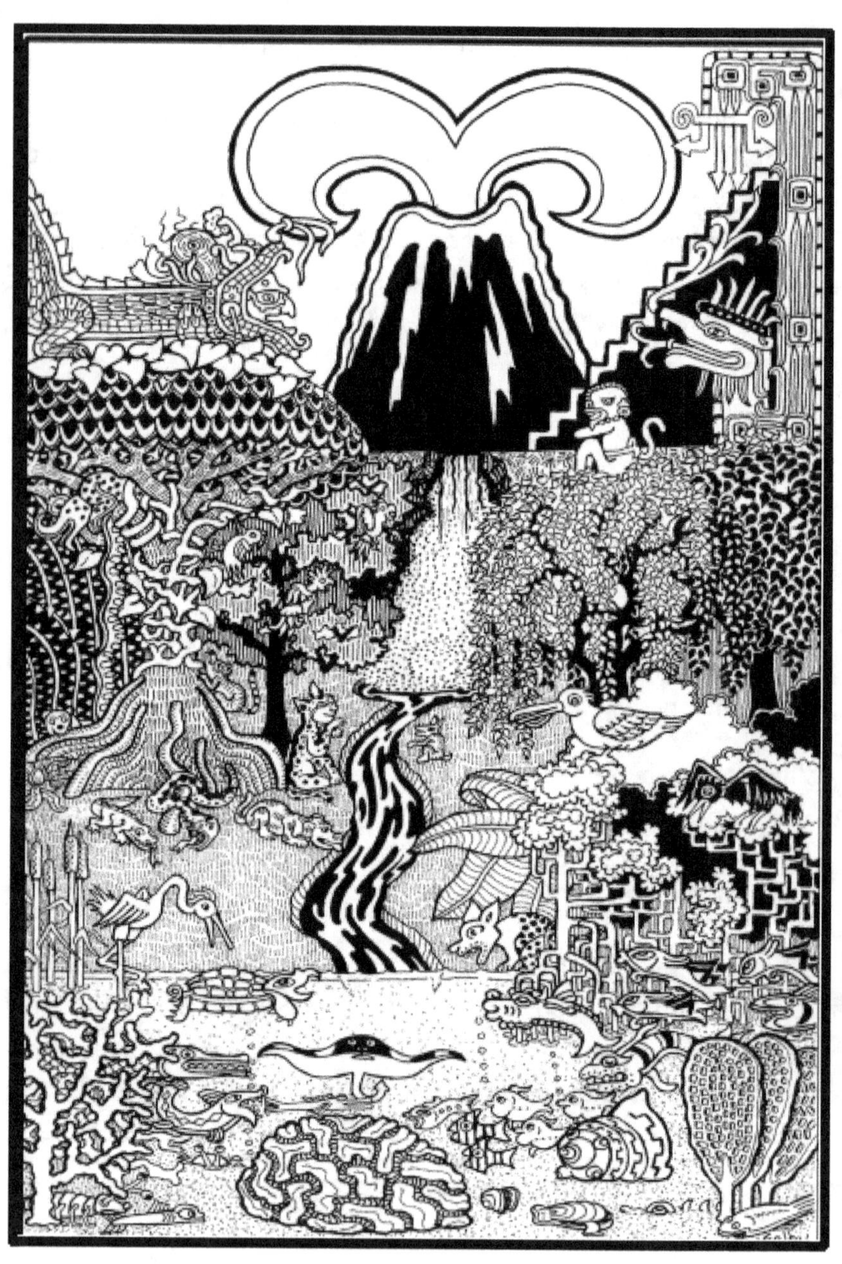

THE DAWN OF ANIMALS

20

Now they rested on a mountaintop and thought and talked of what more they should do. It was decided that what they wanted now was guardians of what they had made. Guardians that would give respect and praise and they would call them animals.

They began by thinking of a form and then naming it and it would come forth. First was the deer and they gave it the canyons and thickets and told it, "to walk on all four legs." Next, they thought of birds in many colors and forms and they told them, "to fly above the earth and sea." Thus, Heart of Earth and Heart of Sky spent much time thinking of and naming the animals, the birds, the fish, the insects, the serpents, and all of the creatures to inhabit this land they had created.

When they had finished they said, "Talk, speak to us. Don't moan, don't cry out. Speak, pray to us, keep our days." But, it didn't turn out that they could speak with their creators. They just chatted or howled or squawked. It was never clear what they were saying. Some of the animals just wanted to crawl off and be by themselves.

Heart of Earth and Heart of Sky conferred with one another and told the animals, "It hasn't turned out the way we hoped, you will simply have to be transformed, you will keep what we have given you but your service will be to be eaten," said the Creators of the earth. What they wanted was something in their image that they could talk with and who would respect them and could understand how things should be. This they called, "the Human Work."

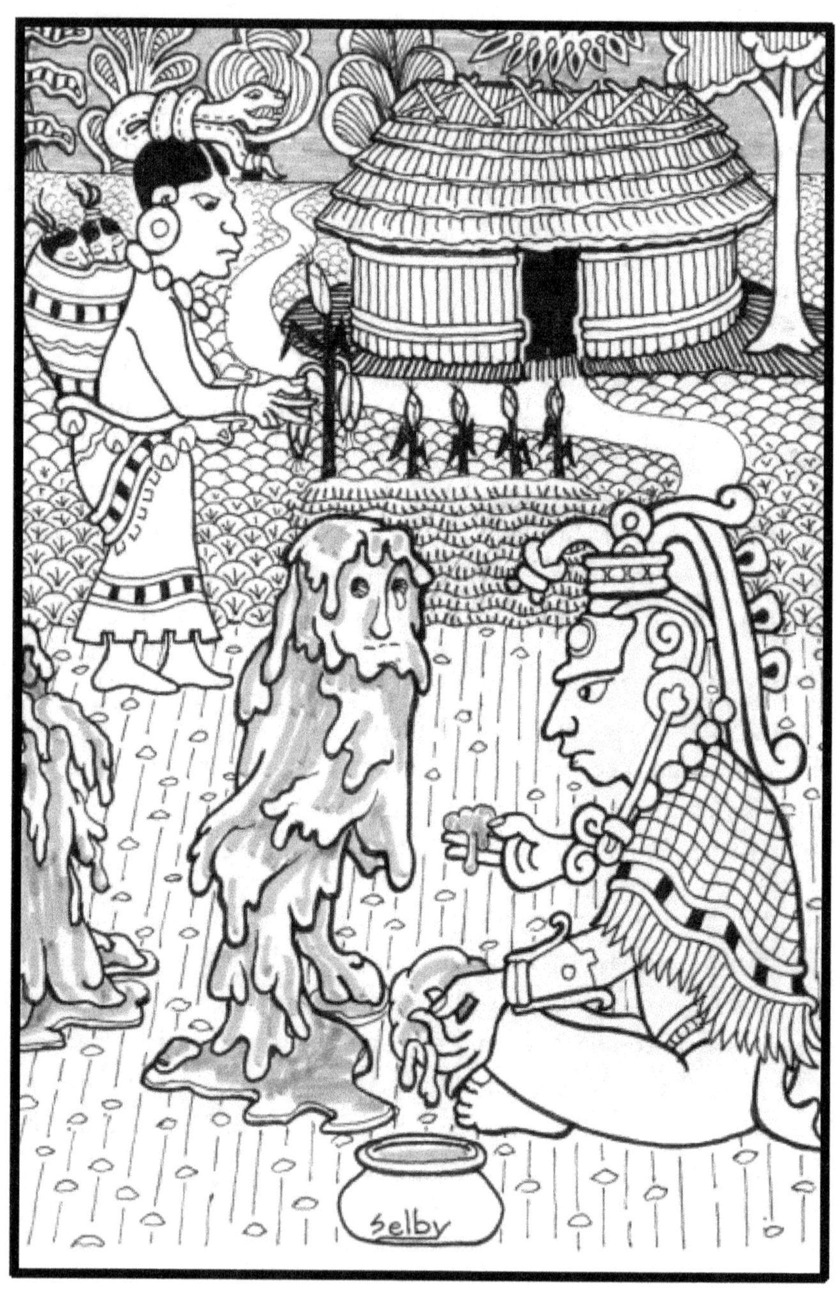

THE FIRST HUMAN WORK

THE FIRST HUMAN WORK

The Creators decided that for this experiment with the Human Work, they needed help. The earth was a large place with much more work to be done and the project of creating Humans would take time so they called forth a Midwife and a Matchmaker, known to this day as grandmother and grandfather of humans.

Heart of Earth and Heart of Sky invoked the daykeepers, diviners, and midmost seers called Xmucane, our grandmother, and Xpiyacoc, our grandfather, to be the providers and nurturers of making the humans. These seers were told to first try earth and mud to make humans. They made human forms but they were just too soft and loose when they were wet and very hard when they dried out and fell apart. When it rained they just dissolved. These first humans couldn't look around, they couldn't walk, and they talked a little but didn't make any sense.

"They won't last," Xmucane and Xpiyacoc, the mason and sculptor of these first humans, said. "It must be tried again. The time for the dawning of the sun, moon, and the heavens is drawing near. If they didn't give praise or respect you must try again," Xmucane and Xpiyacoc were told.

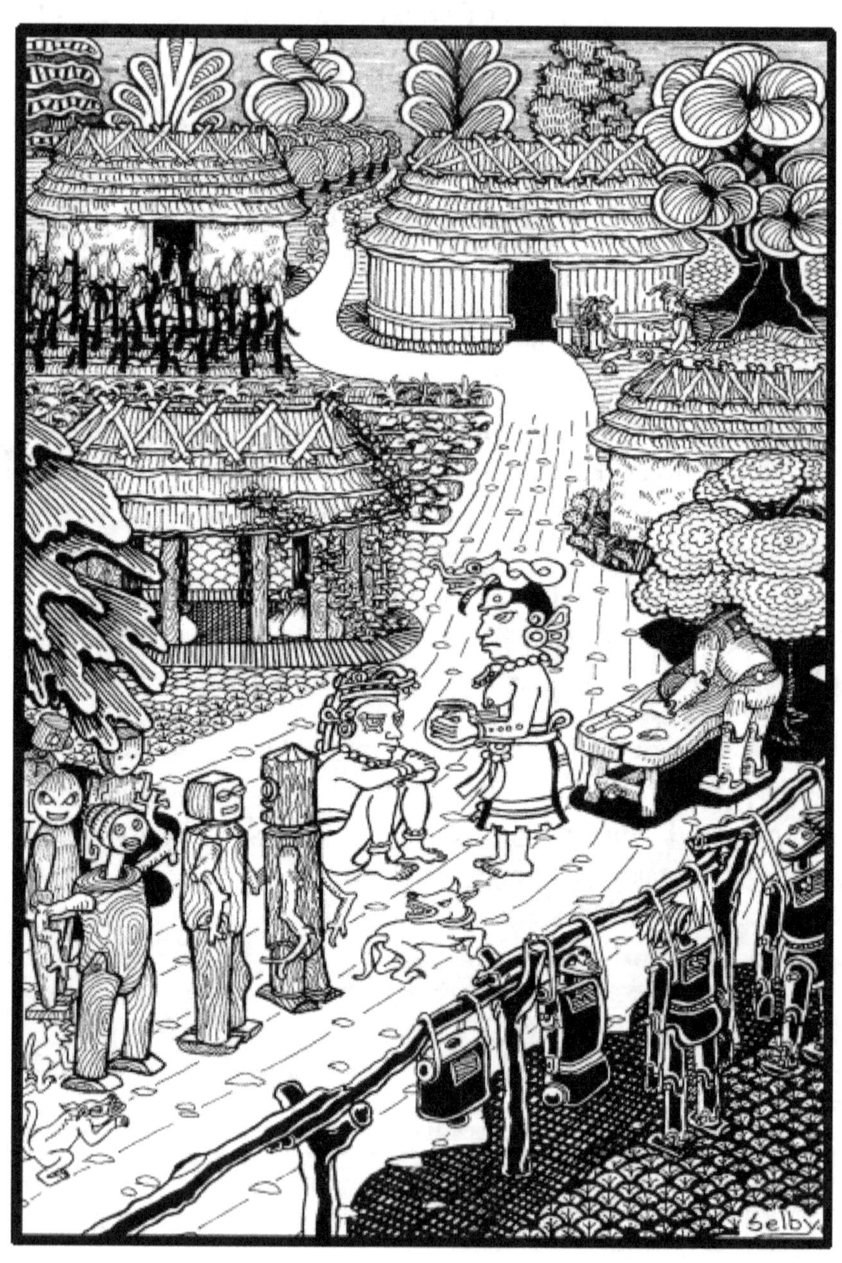

THE SECOND HUMAN WORK

THE SECOND HUMAN WORK

Since clay from the earth didn't work out, Xmucane and Xpiyacoc now have the responsibility to "try again." Their lives must have been very busy during this time with building shelters to live in, cultivating food, and raising two twin boys to be known as One Hunahpu and Seven Hunahpu as well as creating a population of 'humans'.

With the encouragement of the gods they next tried the wood of trees. Xpiyacoc had found, while building their shelters, that some types of very hard stones would cut and shape the wood from trees and the best to work with was the wood from what they call the Croton tree. So he experimented with different shapes and forms to create the first 'wooden People'. Some were wood carvings while others had moving parts and could walk and speak and some could even reproduce themselves.

Slowly a large population was created and they moved freely about the earth but, they had no "heart". They had little ambition and no regard for their home, the Earth they lived on. They were cruel to each other and had no respect for the animals that they shared the Earth with. They had no memory of their creators and remembered nothing of their gods, Heart of Earth and Heart of Sky.

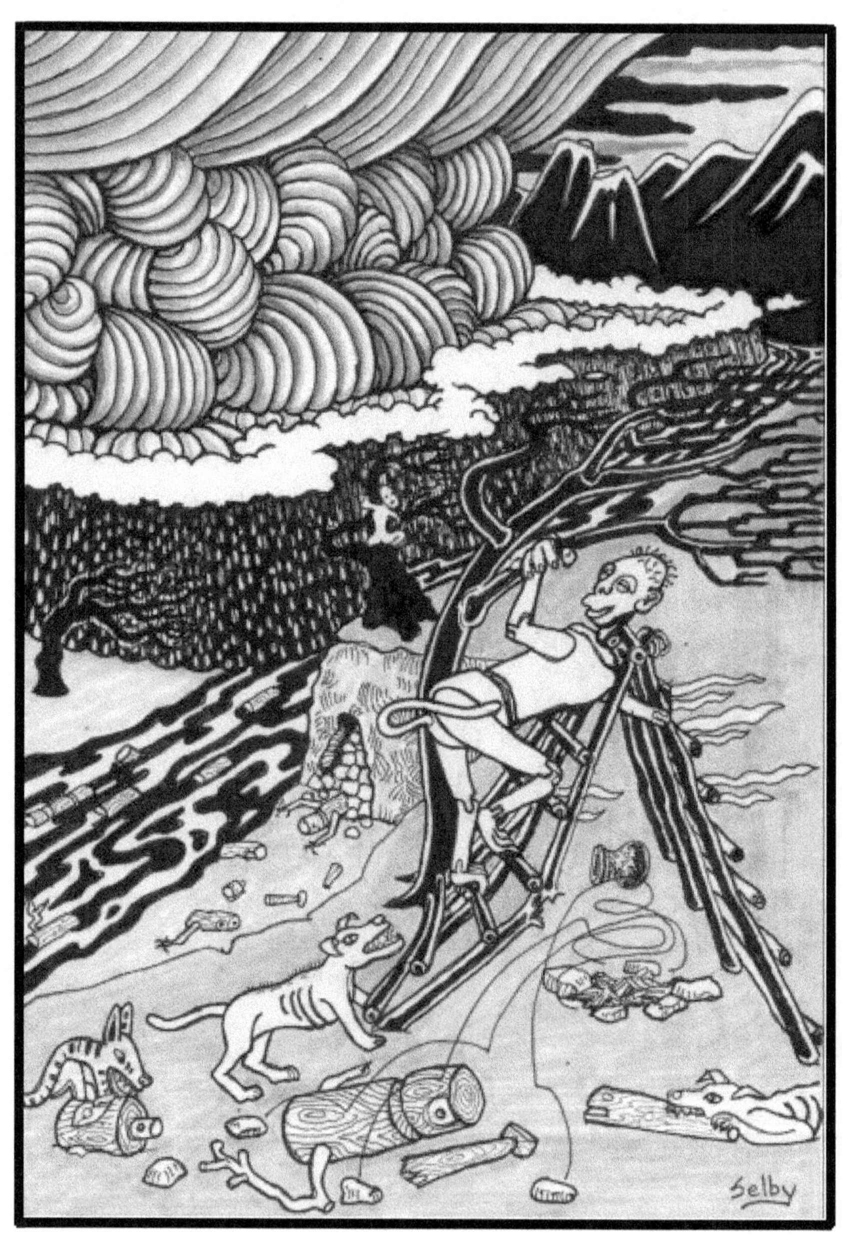

THE FLOOD

THE FLOOD

Everything turned against these manikins and wood carvings. Their dogs attacked them saying, "Why haven't we been fed?" Even the cooking pots and hearth stones threw themselves at them. When they tried to get away and climbed upon the roofs of their shelters the roofs crumbled to the ground. When they ran to caves to get away, the caves dropped stones upon their heads. The animals large and small chased them. Even hot oil and tar fell from the sky to cover them.

And, finally, the Heart of Sky, Hurakan, created huge clouds which swirled and blackened the whole earth bringing thunder and pounding rain and wind for days upon days until the whole earth became covered in water except for the tops of the tallest mountains. The second human work, the second human design had not worked!

But, not all of the wooden people were destroyed. It is said that some of the smaller monkeys in the trees which look like little humans are a sign of this previous human work. A reminder of the human experiments left by Xmucane and Xpiyacoc and the Heart of Sky and Heart of Earth.

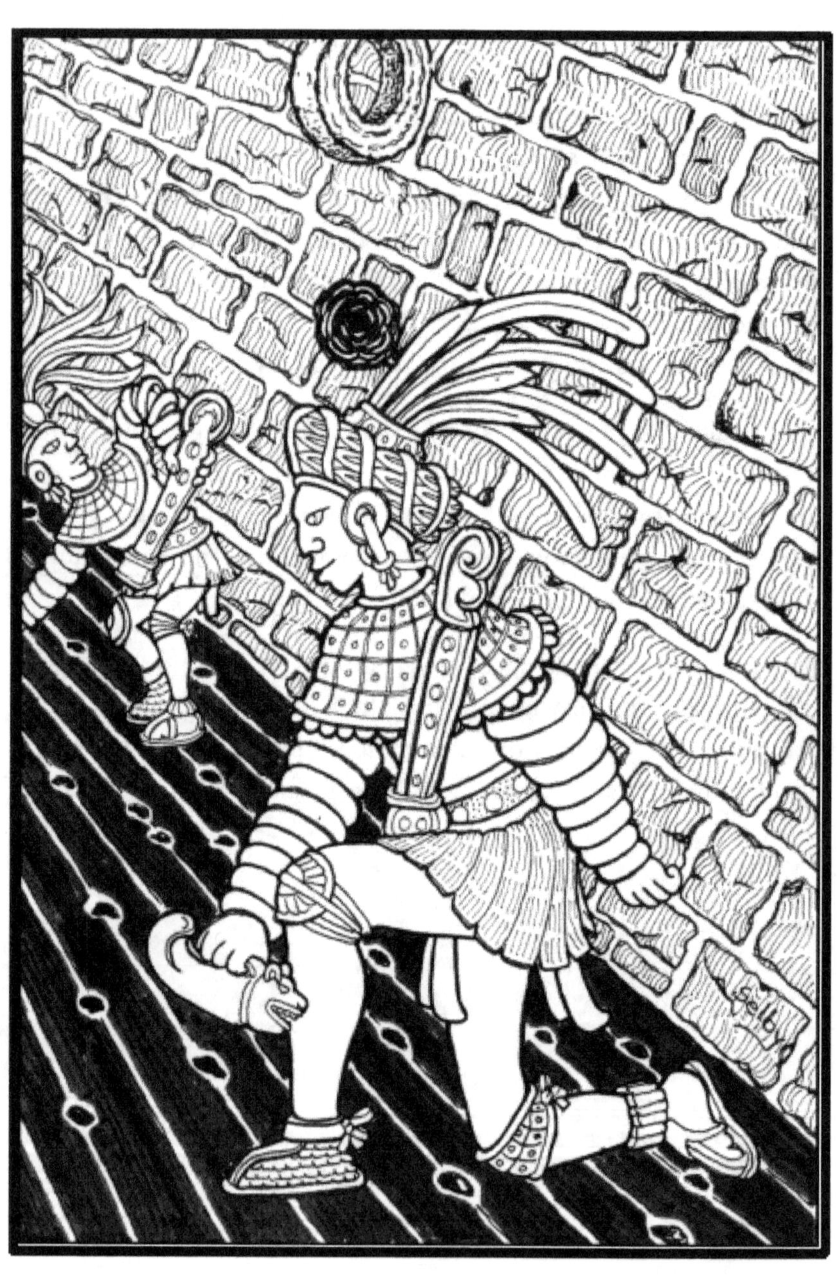

ONE HUNAHPU AND SEVEN HUNAHPU

28

ONE HUNAHPU AND SEVEN HUNAHPU

In the darkness of these early days of the dawning of the earth, Xmucane and Xpiyacoc had twin boys, named One Hunahpu and Seven Hunahpu. They were exceptional thinkers and as wise as their parents. Only One Hunahpu took a wife, Egret Women was her name. She and One Hunahpu also had twin boys named One Monkey and One Artisan.

One Hunahpu and Seven Hunahpu were Seers as their parents were, but had little to do here on earth before the dawning so they mostly threw dice and played ball every day. They did, however, teach the first artistic skills here on earth to one Monkey and One Artisan who became, flutists and drummers, singers and writers, wood and stone carvers, metal and gold workers, potters and jade workers, and of course great ball players.

One and Seven Hunahpu's passion for the ballgame was great and they played each other whenever they could as One Hunahpu's children grew they had many spritted games together. They made protective clothing and introduced rubber balls and became very accomplished at getting the ball through the eye of the goal stone.

Often when they gathered in the ball court to play a falcon would come to watch them. This falcon was the messenger of Hurakan who enjoyed hearing of the activities of his seers and the progress of the earth and its animals. And as for the falcon, it wasn't far to the earth nor was it far to Xibalba. He could get back to Hurakan in a moment with the latest news.

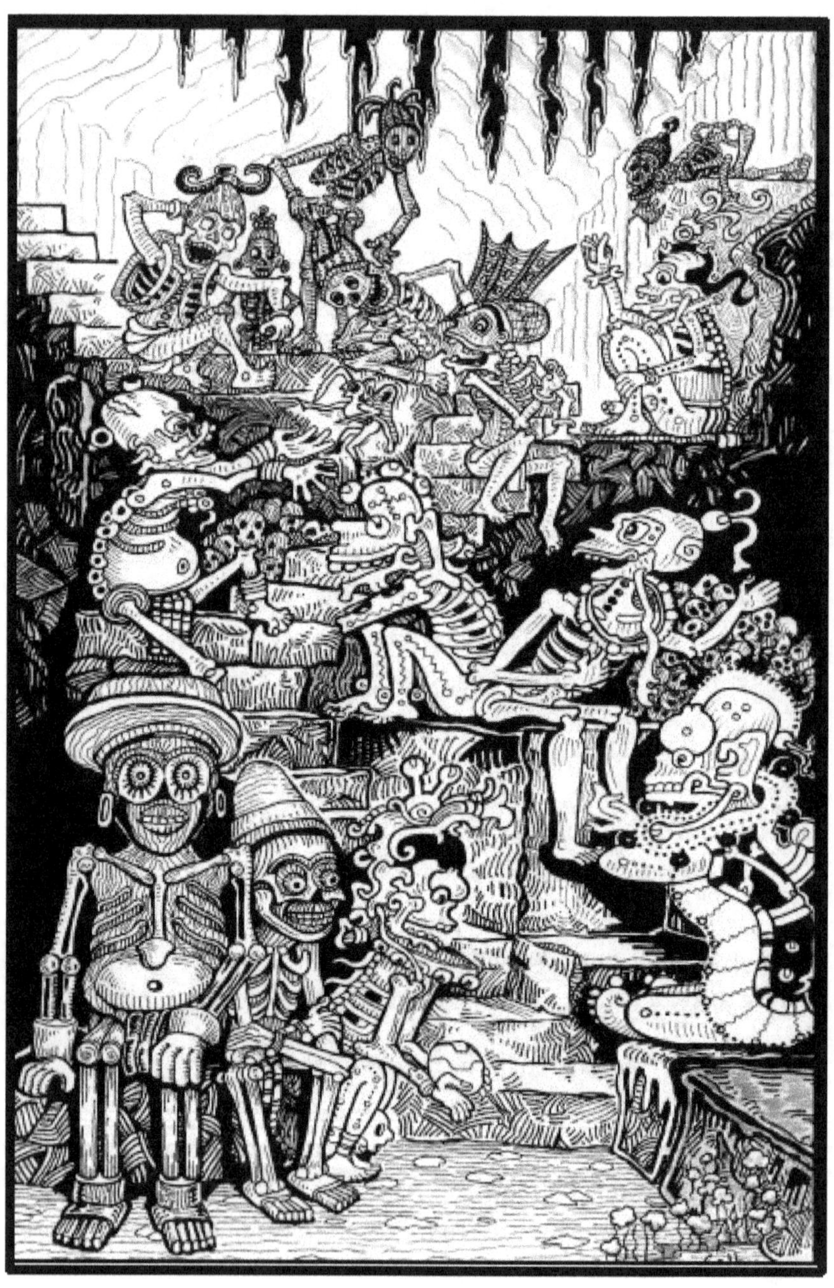

XIBALBA

XIBALBA

Xibalba, 'the place of fear' is the Maya Underworld and it just happened to be under the ball court that one and Seven Hunahpu had built and loved to play at so often. It seems that Heart of Earth and Heart of Sky conceived Xibalba as a cave of many chambers for the future resting place for humans after death. It may have been more than that since the sun and moon and some of the planets would have to have a way through the earth to return to the East to rise in the day or night sky. As in the rest of the world the Maya did not realize what the sky was and how the earth and plants circle the sun yet they were extraordinary dedicated watchers of the heavens.

At this point in the Popol Vuh, our stories shift towards Xibalba so let's meet the important 'Lords of the Underworld' and their commissions:

One Death and Seven Death - the leaders of Xibalba

Scab Stripper and Blood Gather - draw blood from people

Demon of Pus and Demon of Jaundice - make pus/jaundice

Bone Scepter and Skull Scepter - emancipation and edema

Demon of Filth and Demon of Woe punish filth in the home

Wing and Backpack - death on the road or sudden death

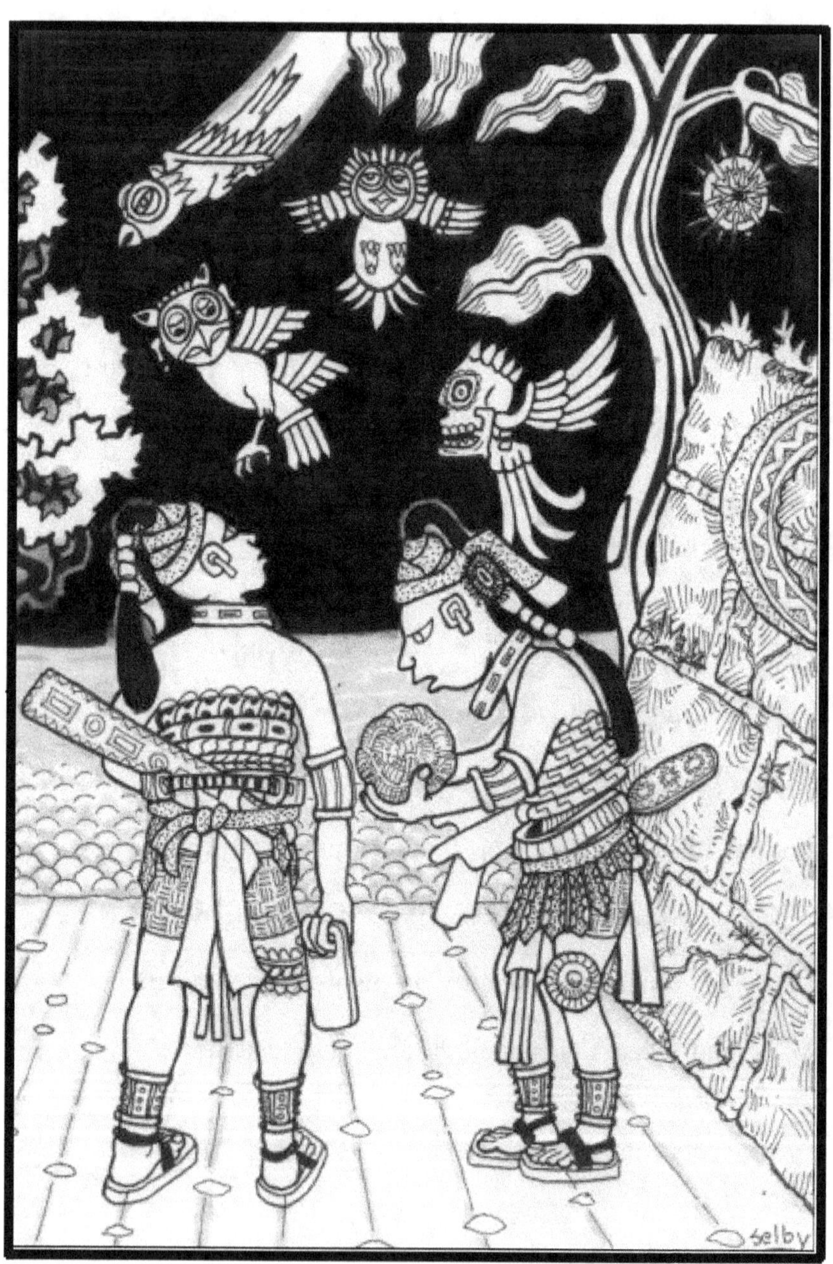

SUMMONED TO XIBALBA

SUMMONED TO XIBALBA

One day, with not much to do, One and Seven Death heard One and Seven Hunahpu playing ball above them and they said to each other, "What is happening on the face of the Earth? All that shouting and stomping. They should be summoned to play ball here." When they shared their thoughts with the other Lords they all agreed to send for them, What the Xibalbans wanted was One and Seven Hunahpu's ball-playing gear; their kilts, their yokes, their arm guards, their panuchos, and headbands.

So the Xibalbans called for their Owl Messengers which were:

Shooting Owl - like a point, just piercing

One-legged Owl - with one leg but has wings

Macaw Owl - with a red back, he has wings

Skull Owl - with only a skull but with wings

These are the messengers of the Underworld who flew quickly to the ballcourt called, "Great Hollow with Fish in the Ashes," where One and Seven Hunahpu were playing ball on their own. The Owls repeated their instructions and told the boys that they 'must' go, "Right away" and "Oh, bring your gaming equipment!"

"Very well, but wait for us while we notify our mother," they replied.

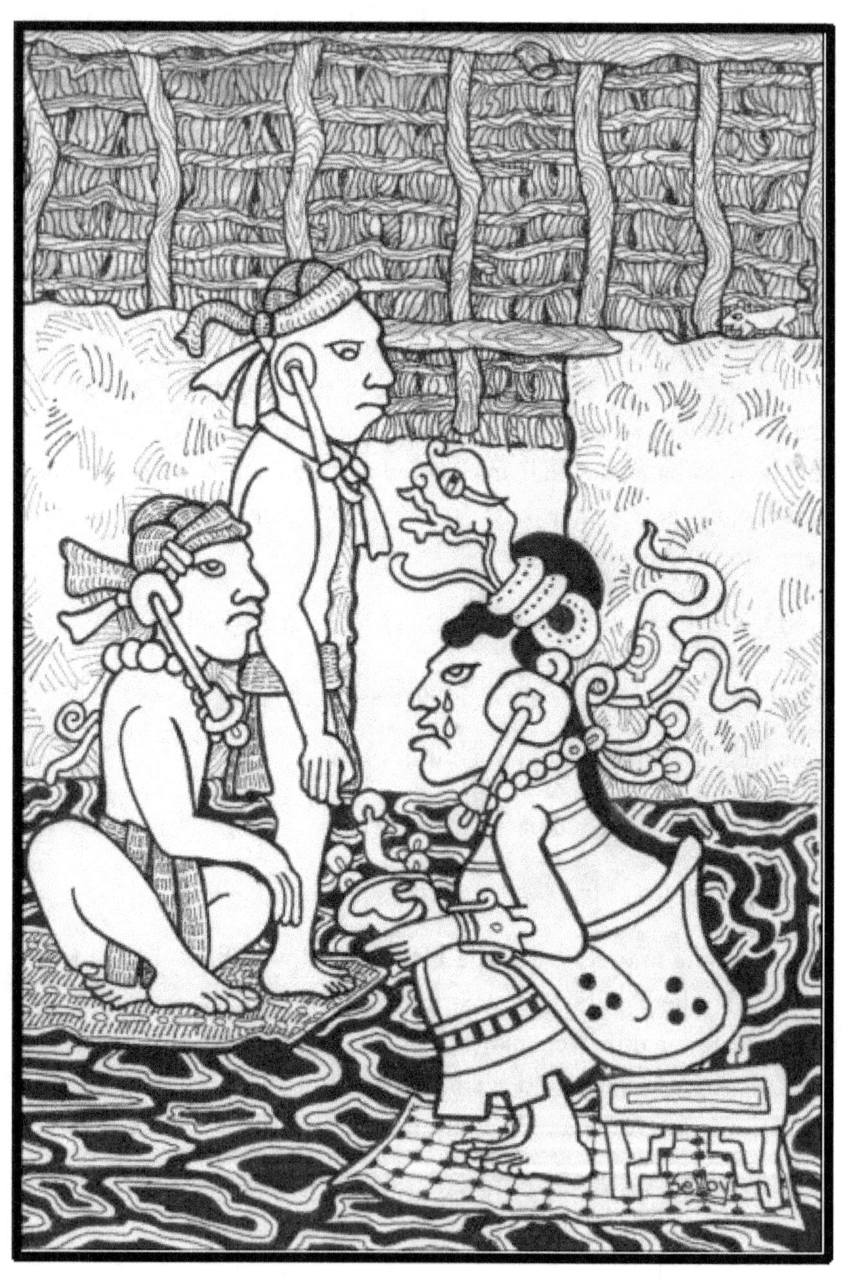

THE LEAVING

THE LEAVING

They went to their house and told their mother, Xmucane, and we must assume One Hunahpu's wife, Egret Woman, what had happened. Xmucane sobbed and was very upset. We don't know what Xmucane knew about Xibalba or One and Seven Death but most likely she was aware of the danger that faced her sons.

The boys changed out of their ball game equipment and told One Monkey and One Artisan to carefully hide their gaming equipment in the roof space of their house. They also asked the boys to look after their mother and grandmother and to play, and sing and write to keep them occupied while they were gone. They didn't expect to be gone very long.

They then told their mother, "We're going. We're not dying so don't be sad!" They then left with the Owls for Xibalba.

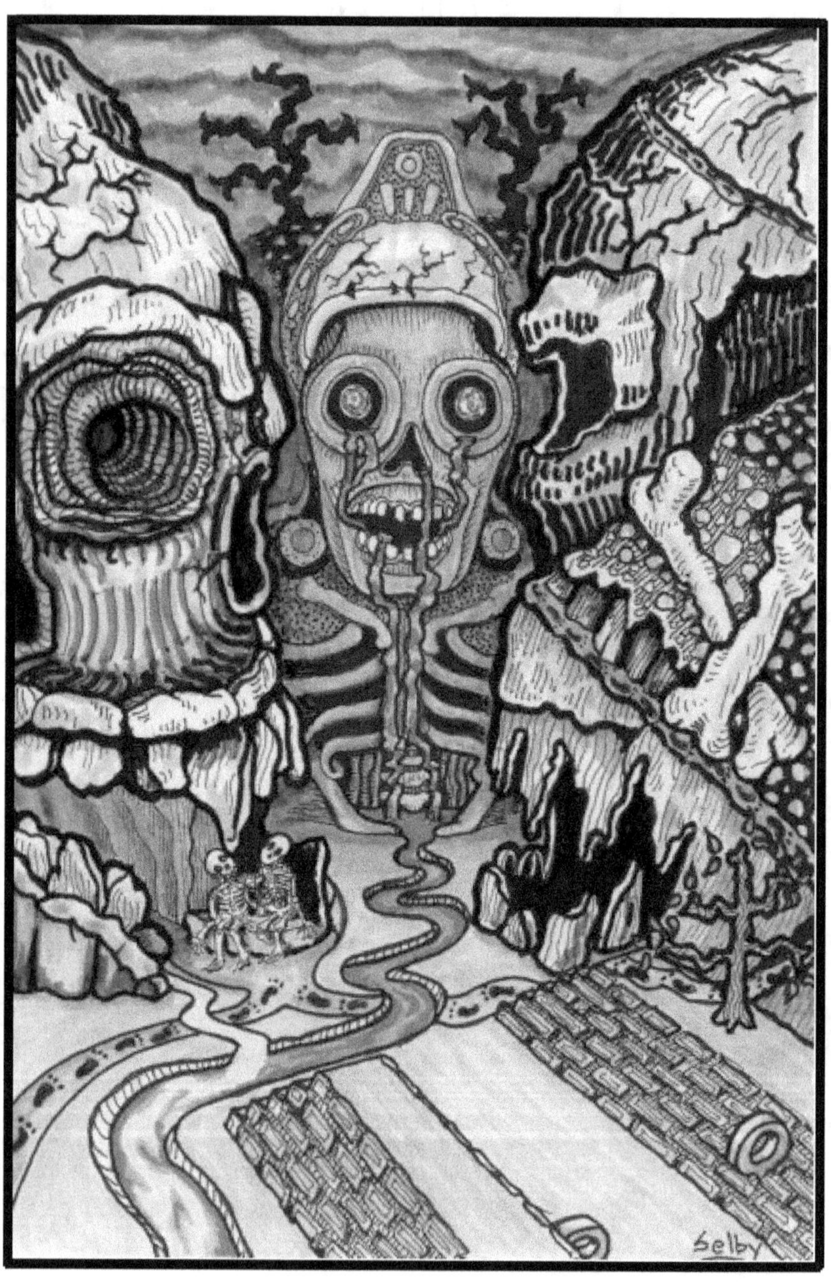

Selby

JOURNEY TO XIBALBA

JOURNEY TO XIBALBA

The boys then descended the road to Xibalba, going down a steep slope where Rustling Canyon and Gurgling Canyon meet at Scorpion Rapids. They were able to pass through the mass of Scorpions without being stung by wrapping their feet in banana leaves. Next was Blood River and then a river of pus where they found poles to cross the river on.

They then came to the Crossroads and they were defeated there. Xibalba has many tests for the would-be visitors as you will see. At the Crossroads there is a Red Road, a Black Road, a White Road, and a Yellow Road. They did not know which to take and the owls knew but would not help them in a planned effort to defeat them.

In time, the Black Road spoke, "I am the one you should take. I am the Lord's road." So they were defeated. They did not know which road to take.

Once again on the move, they descended a very steep path to a deep gorge where strange cliffs seemed to be waiting for them. Most of the rocks were black, while bone-white outcrops of rock formed skull-like heads. Deep caves in the stone seemed to be large black eyes that followed their every movement. Even stranger was the ballcourt set in the middle of the floor of the gorge made from blood-red stone. Along one side of the court was the 'Place of the Ball Game Sacrifice' with its scattered graves and Sacrificial Stone. In the middle stood a dead tree. The two boys could see no other plants while a heavy gloom hung over the gorge like a shroud.

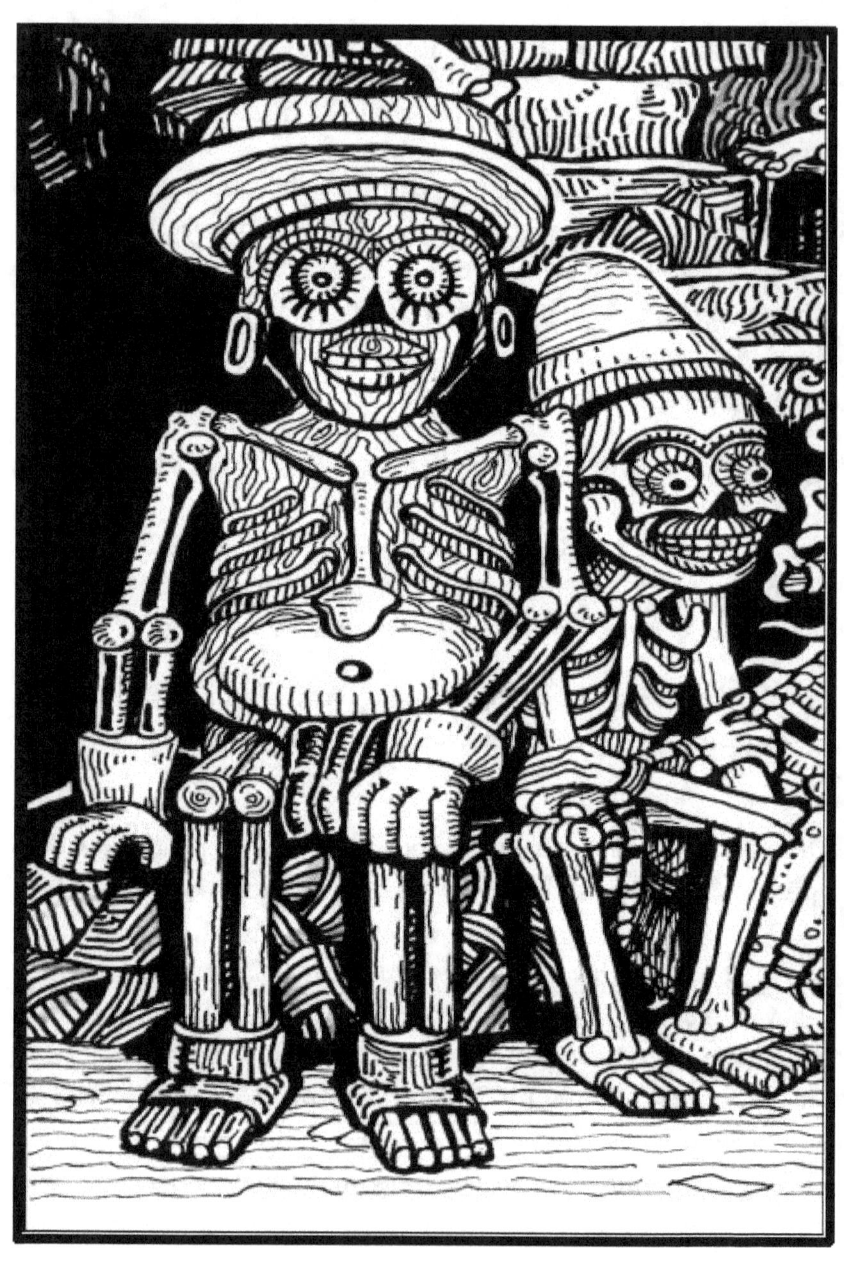

THE MANIKINS

THE MANIKINS

The owls showed them to a large entrance on the stone cliff that looked much like a large mouth with hanging teeth. Here the owls left them to enter the council chamber of the lords of Xibalba, alone. As their eyes adjusted to the darkness they made out the form of two lords and wanting to be polite they greeted them by saying, "Evening, One Death," "Evening, Seven Death". They were defeated yet again! In Xibalba, they have put two manikins for just this purpose.

All of the Lords of Xibalba just broke up laughing and shouting. They were so pleased with themselves.

Finally, the lord seated closest to the manikins said, "It is good that you have come. Tomorrow you must put on your ball game equipment and we will play ball but, for now just have a seat here on this bench and rest" they were told. The bench was a burning hot rock. They sat but not for long while all of the lords laughed and shouted and shricked until their bones hurt. Never had they had so much fun!

Next, they were told that they could sleep in a "Dark House" where there was never any light. They were given each a cigar and one pine torch and told that in the morning they must return them "unused!"

This of course is the first test of the houses of Xibalba. Not knowing better they lit the torches and cigars.

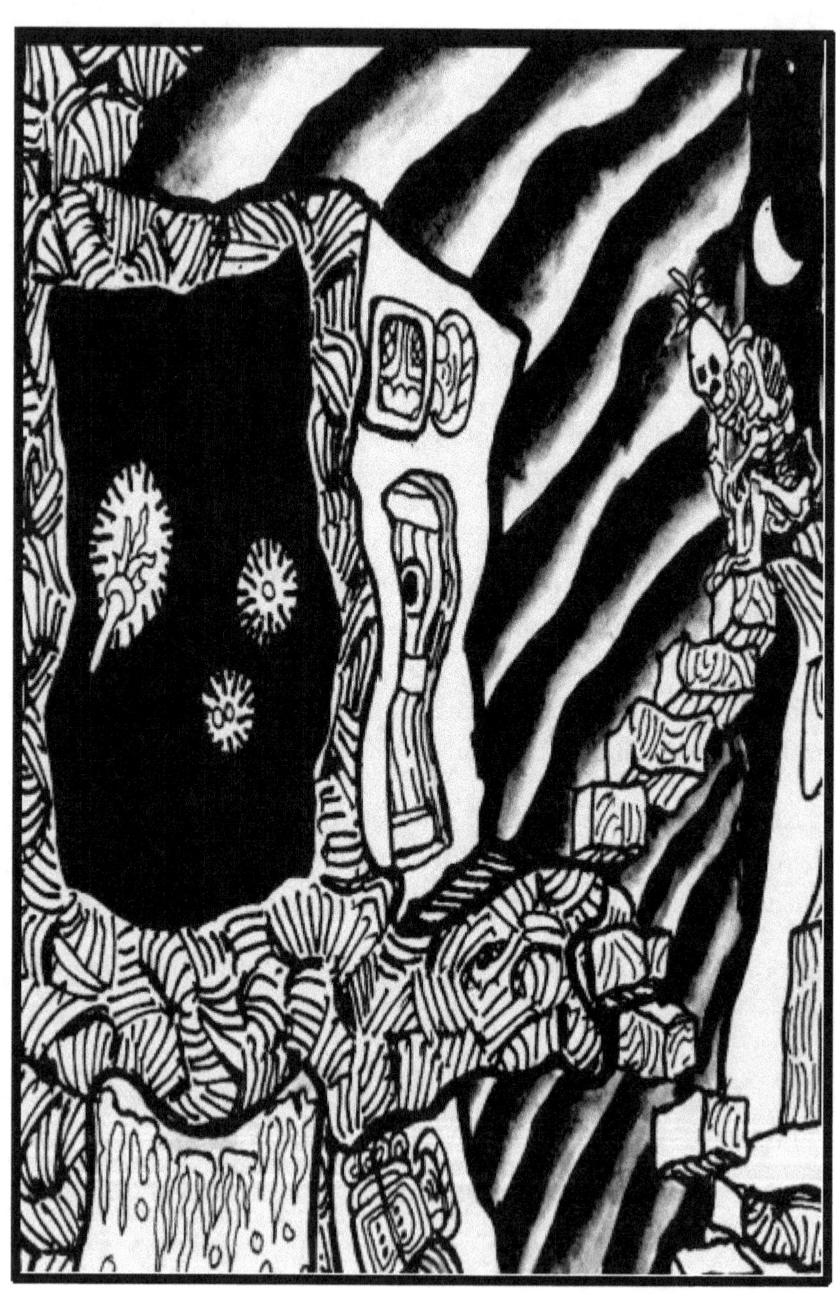

LORDS OF XIBALBA

In the morning when One and Seven Hunahpu were called before One and Seven Death, they were asked where the torch and cigars had gone. They answered that they had used them because the room was so dark.

"Very well," said One Death, "This very day you will die. You are both finished. You will disappear. You will be sacrificed. You have failed a test in Xibalba."

And that morning they were sacrificed and buried in a place called, "Place of the Ball Game Sacrifice." The head of One Hunahpu was cut off and placed in the fork of the old dead tree that stands by the road there. When his head was put in the fork of the tree a very strange thing happened. Within minutes fruit began to grow and by noon of that same day, most of the tree was covered in large round objects very much like the head of One Hunahpu.

This is the tree that is now known as the Calabash tree or the 'Tree of the Skull of One Hunahpu" as it is said.

No one had seen such a thing in Xibalba or anywhere else. One and Seven Death were amazed and they told all of the Xibalbans who wanted to see this strange thing that they should not pick or taste the fruit. This was something that they could not understand. How could One Hunahpu's head make this old tree bear fruit and what had become of One Hunahpu's head because no one could pick it out? They all looked the same.

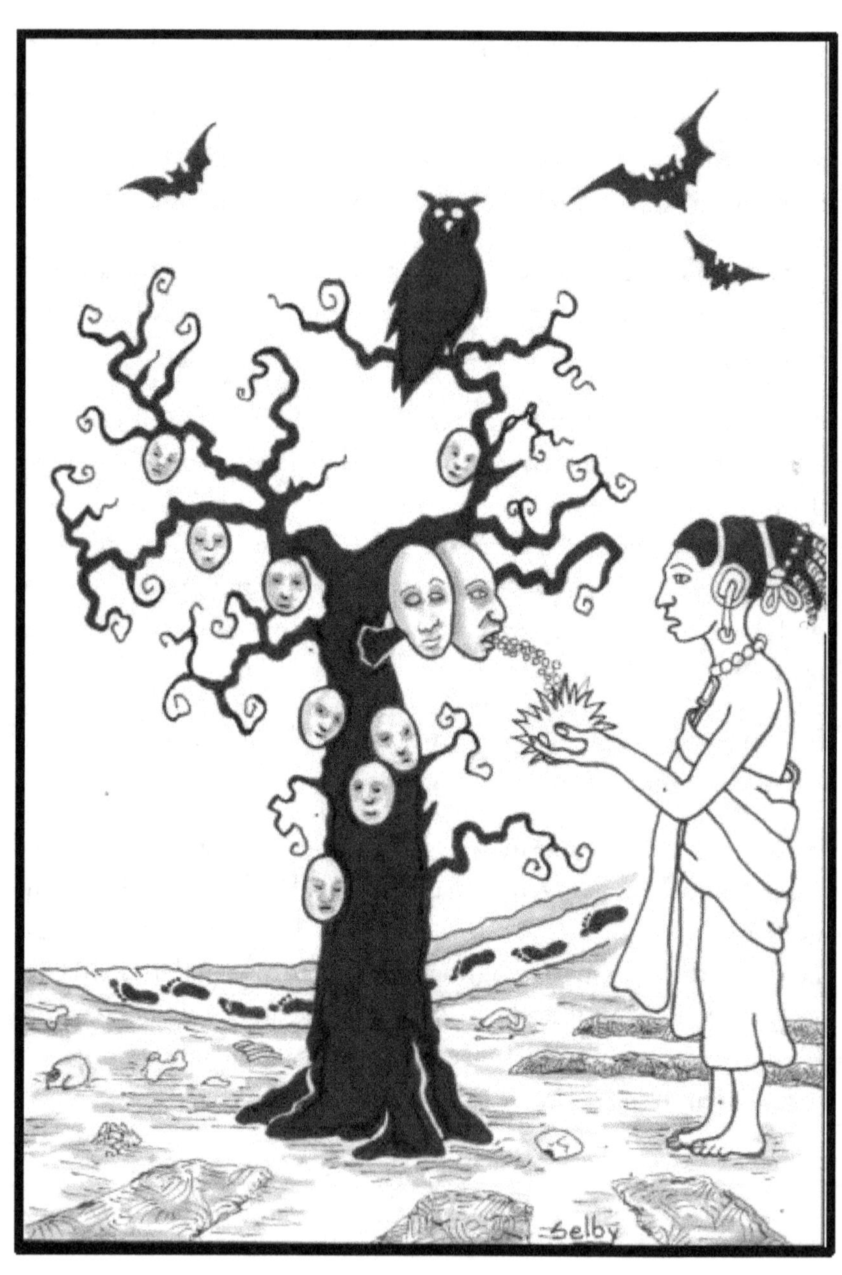

BLOOD MOON

BLOOD MOON

The fourth Lord of Xibalba was named Blood Gatherer and he had a young daughter called Blood Moon. Blood Moon had heard what had happened with the old tree beside the path next to the Place of Ball Game Sacrifice and went to see for herself. She had heard that the fruit was truly sweet and she thought she might try it.

As she stood next to the tree she said to herself, "If the fruit is truly sweet it should not be wasted."

Then something spoke to her from the branches of the tree. "Why do you want a mere bone, a round thing in the branches of an old tree?"

"I do want it!" said the maiden.

"Very well. Stretch out your right hand here so I can see it," said the bone. And when she did this, the bone spits out saliva into her hand. When she looked at her hand the saliva was no longer there.

The bone then said, "A father does not disappear, rather, he will leave his daughters and sons. So it is that I have done likewise through you."

After six months her father noticed that she was with child. When he spoke of this with One and Seven Death they said make her talk. "Very well, your Lordships," he replied and went to question his daughter.

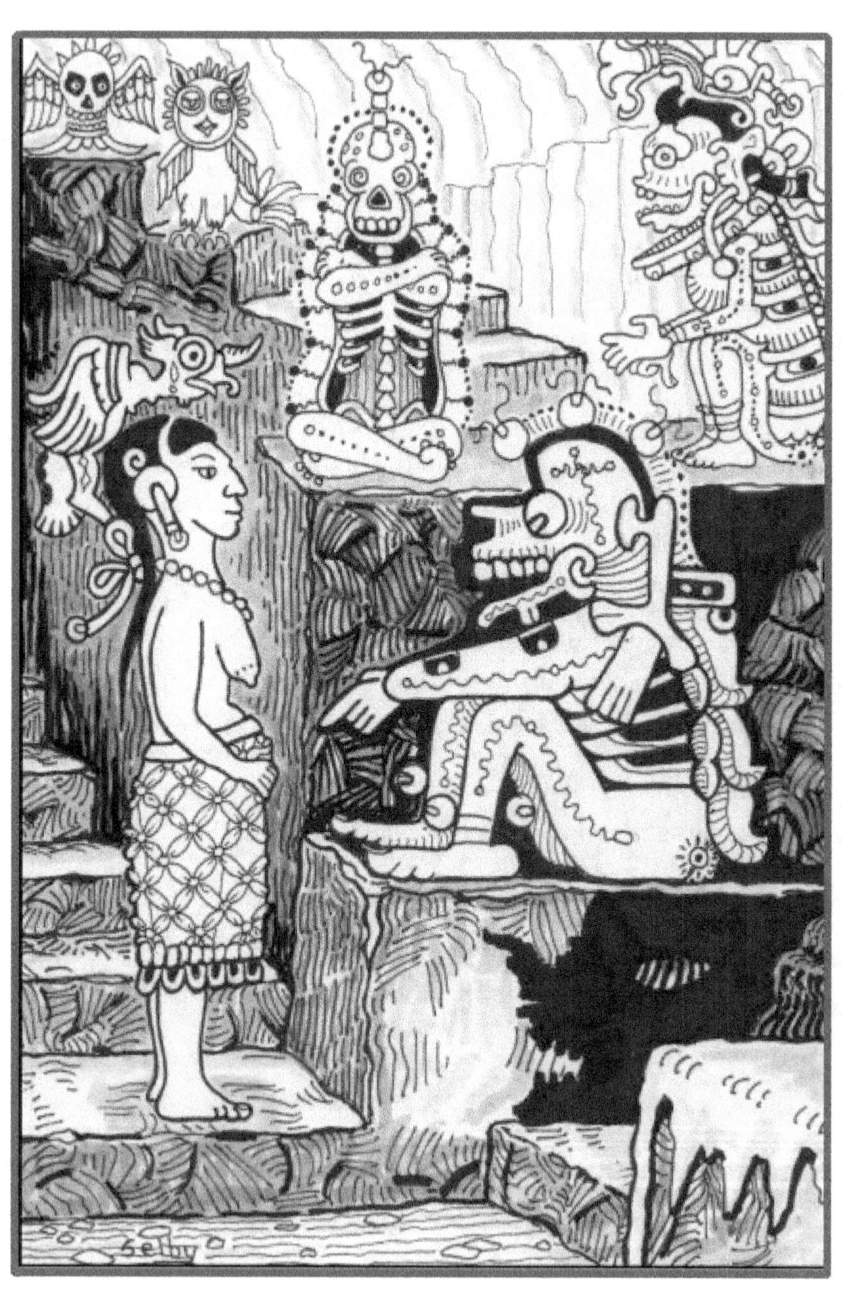

BLOOD MOON TO BE SACRIFICED

BLOOD MOON TO BE SACRIFICED

Who is responsible for the child in your body?" her father asked while One and Seven Death watched.

"There is no child, my father, there is no man whose face I have known," she replied.

When One Death turned his thumb down her father said, "Very well, It is a bastard you carry." Turning to the owls he said, "Take her away for sacrifice. Bring back her heart in a bowl, so that the lords can take it in their hands this very day."

The owls and Blood Moon then left carrying the bowl along with the white dagger the instrument of sacrifice. "It will not turn out well if you try to sacrifice me, my messengers, because it is not a bastard that I carry. What is in my belly comes from the Heart of Earth and Heart of Sky through One and Seven Hunahpu. The child is meant to be born," said the maiden.

"What are we going to use in place of her heart? What should we deliver in the bowl? What we want most is that you should not die!" said the owl messengers.

"Very well. My heart must not be theirs, nor will your home always be here. I will gather for you the red sap of the Croton tree in your bowl and we will let it dry for a while and then form it into the shape of a heart and then cover it with fresh red sap," explained Blood Moon. "Very well maiden. We'll show you the way to the surface. Just wait for us, we must deliver this duplicate, first," the owls told her.

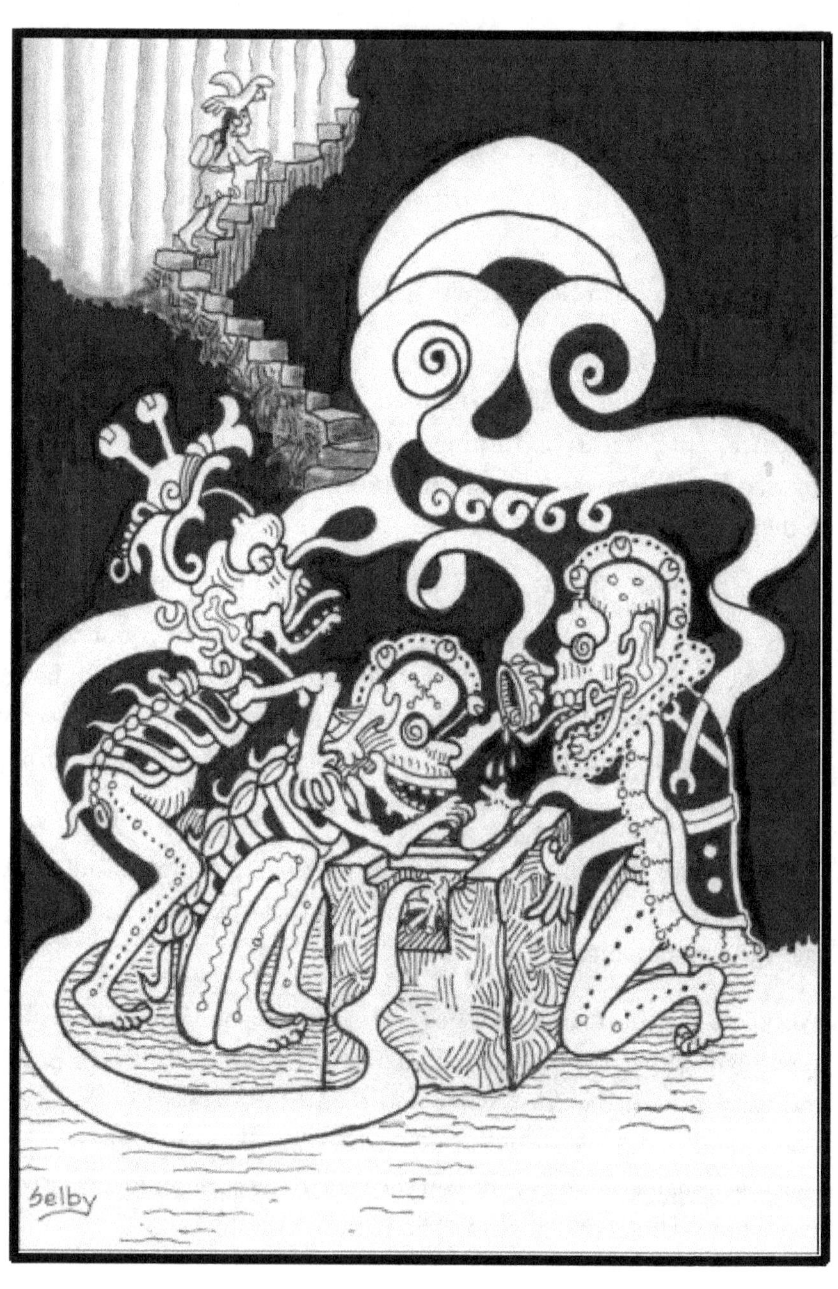

BLOOD MOON DEFEATS THE LORDS

46

BLOOD MOON DEFEATS THE LORDS

When the owls came before the Lords they were watched closely. "Hasn't it turned out well?" asked One Death.

"It has turned out well, your lordships, this is her heart here in the bowl," replied Shooting Owl who was afraid his nervousness was showing.

"Very well," said One Death slowly. "I will have a look." He lifted it up with his fingers, its surface was thick with gore and glistening red like blood. After a moment he made what might have been a smile and said, "Wonderful, stir up the fire and we will dry it out a little.

As the three lords of Xibalba leaned over what they thought to be the cooking heart of Blood Moon, the sweet aroma of the Croton tree drove them ecstatic. Their thoughts swarmed with the anticipation of the warm heart to be shared and they noticed not that the owls were leading Blood Moon to the upper world and the house of Xmucane.

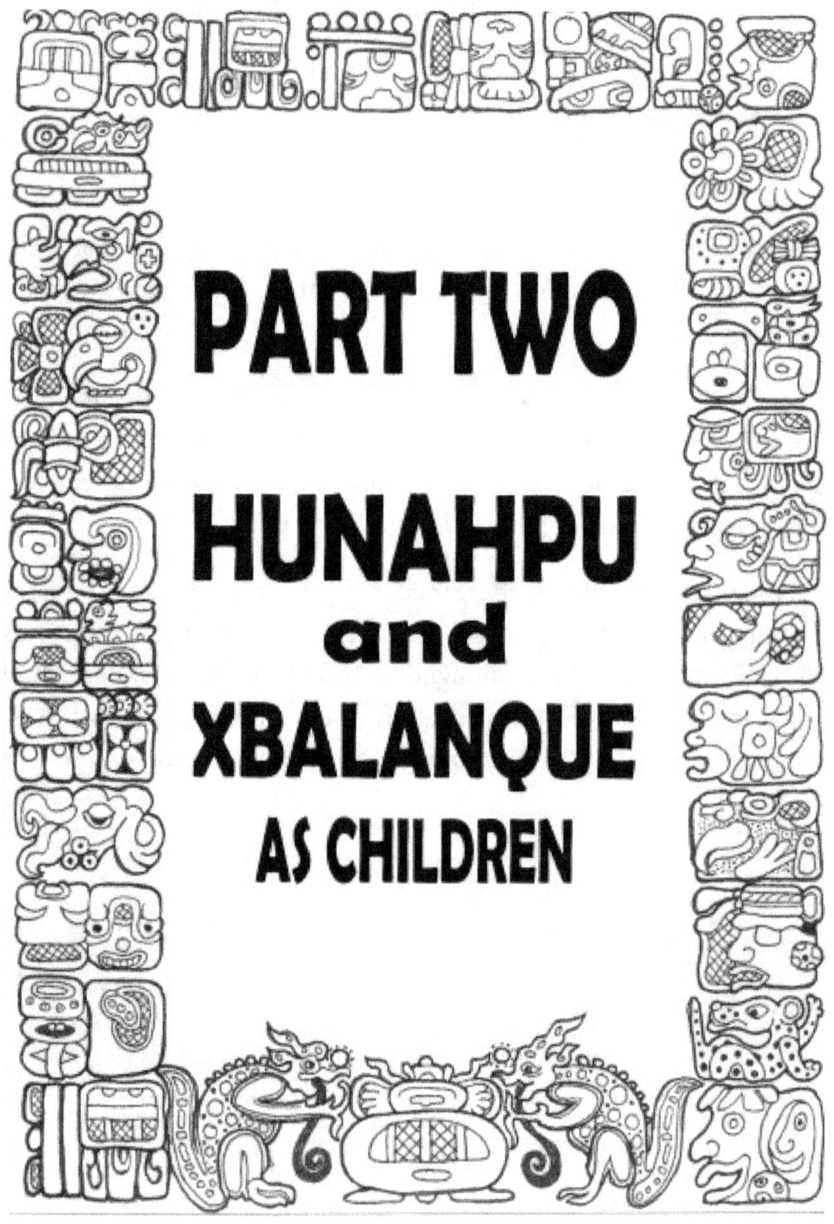

PART TWO

HUNAHPU
and
XBALANQUE
AS CHILDREN

PART TWO

49

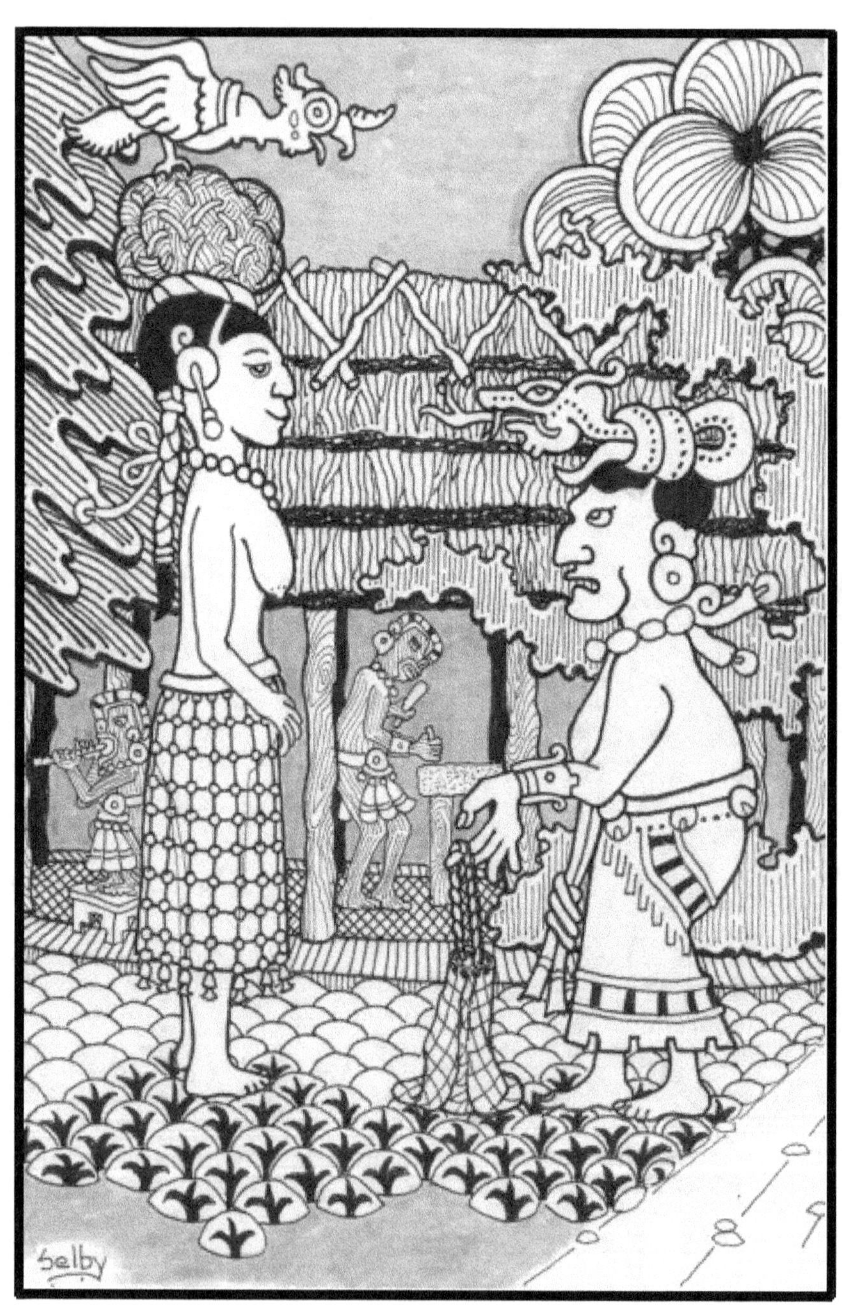

BLOOD MOON MEETS XMUCANE

BLOOD MOON MEETS XMUCANE

When Blood Moon meets Xmucane she is six months with a child. By this time Xmucane did know what had happened to her children, One and Seven Hunahpu but, the grandmother did not believe her account of what had happened to Blood Moon at the old tree in the Place of the Ball Game Sacrifice.

"I don't want you, no thanks, my 'daughter-in-law.' It's just a bastard in your belly, you trickster! These children of mine that you have named are dead," Xmucane said.

"Even so I am your daughter-in-law. One and Seven Hunahpu are not dead and have merely made a way for the light of the dawning to show itself as you will see when you look at the faces of what I bear," she told Xmucane.

"Truly what I say to you is true."

The two women stood looking at each other while Xmucane began to think that perhaps it was true what this stranger was saying. She then devised a test to see if the girl was telling the truth.

"Very well, my daughter-in-law, I hear You. So get going and pick a netful of ripe corn, my daughter in law. Get some food so you and the child can eat," the maiden was told.

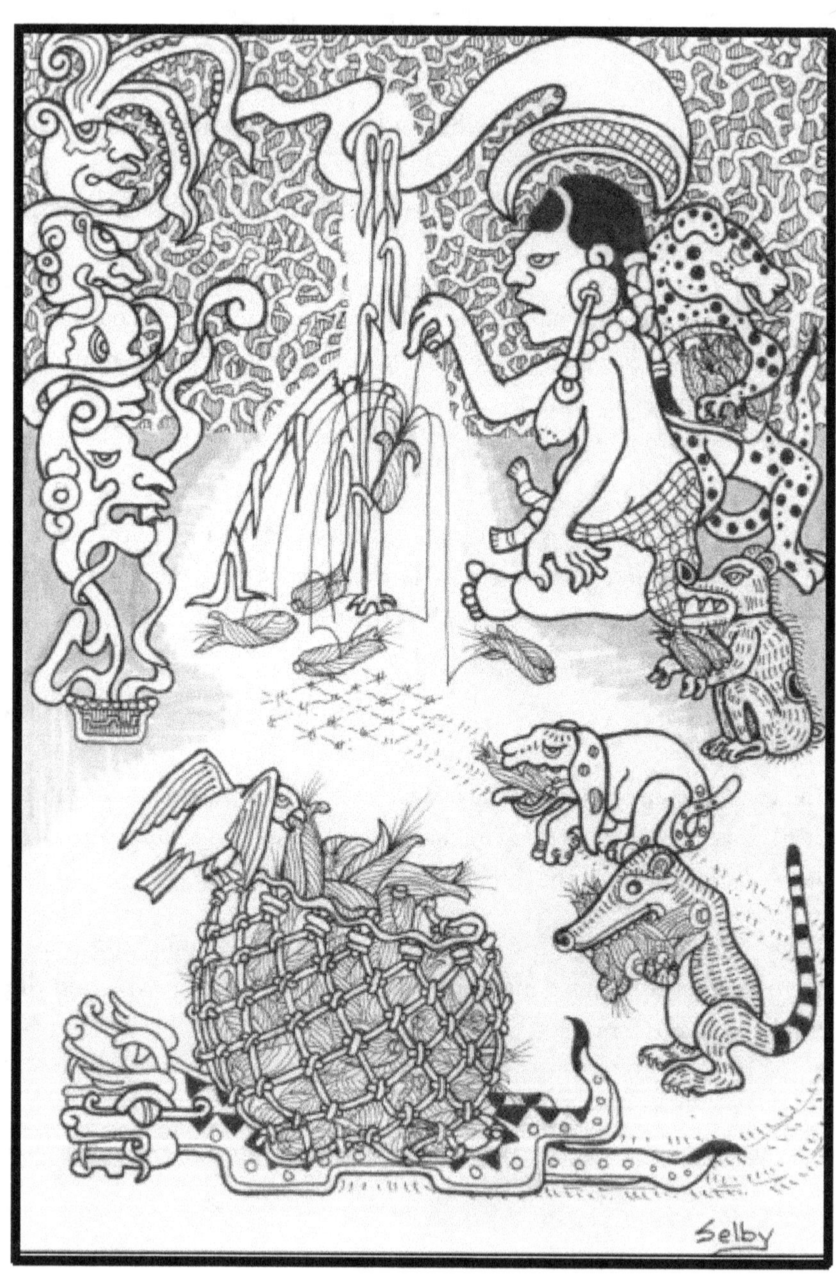

BLOOD MOON COLLECTS CORN

BLOOD MON COLLECTS CORN

After that, Blood Moon went to the garden of One Monkey and One Artisan but the garden had only one dried clump of corn that had but one ear. "How can I get a netful of corn from this," she thought and then she knew.

She found a small amount of dried sap from the croton tree and lit it while calling upon the guardians of food,

"Come on out, rise now, come on out, stand up now;

Thunder Woman, Yellow Woman,

Cacao Woman, Cornmeal Women,

Thou guardians of food."

And then she took hold of the silk, the bunch of silk at the top of the ear. She just pulled out one strand but didn't pick the ear and the ear reproduced enough fresh ears to fill the net. Then all the animals came to help her collect the ears to fill the net and carry the net.

When the grandmother saw the full net in the cookhouse she rushed off to see if the whole garden had been picked clean. But, when she sees the condition of the garden she knows that her grandsons have done little to maintain it. When she sees the mark of the net on the ground she knows that Blood Moon was no trickster but much more. Xmucane knows how to read the counting of days and that 'net' is the day Venus will rise as the morning star, the imprint of the net in the field she takes this as a sign that the sons of Blood Moon will make this possible.

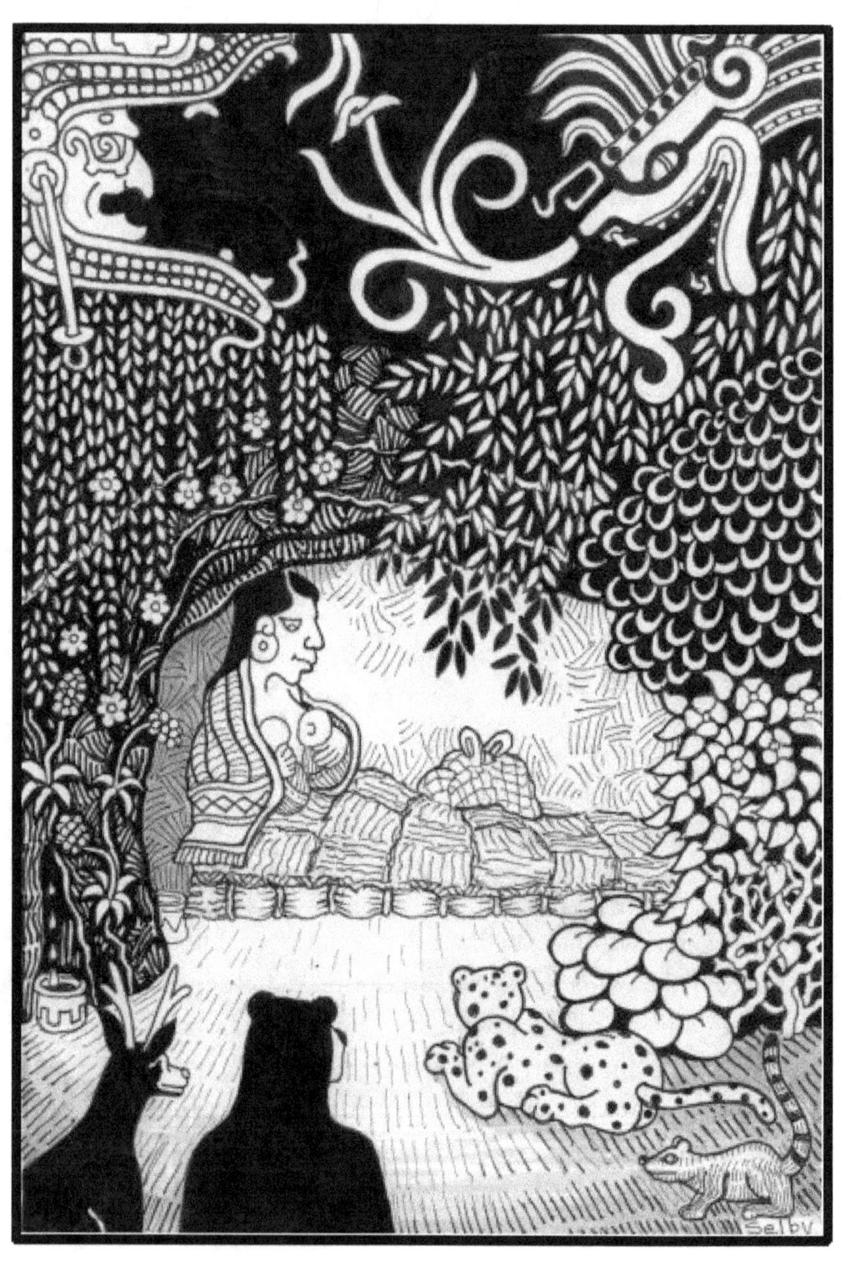

THE BIRTH OF HUNAHPU AND XBALANQUE

THE BIRTH OF HUNAHPU AND XBALANQUE

Blood Moon didn't spend much time with Xmucane and her grandsons before she gave birth. She had spent all of her life up to this time in the caves of Xibalba and preferred the mountains where small caves sheltered her as she was accustomed to. As a child she had played with the owls and other animals in the underworld and here in the mountains were many animals that would help her. Her life though hard was comfortable and would provide a wonderful place for her children to grow up.

The owls came to visit often and brought her news of Xibalba but she didn't miss her life there and had no desire to return. Her friends had all been animals and the Water Lilly Jaguar was her favorite but here the animals were very friendly and she spoke often to them.

When Blood Moon was due, one night she quickly gave birth to twin boys, Hunahpu and Xbalanque. The boys were very strong and grew fast as she expected them too. However, they didn't seem to sleep much so when she felt strong enough she decided to take them to their grandmother so she would know that what she had spoken was true. She wove them soft blankets and tied them over her shoulders so one was on each side of her breast and she set off to see Xmucane.

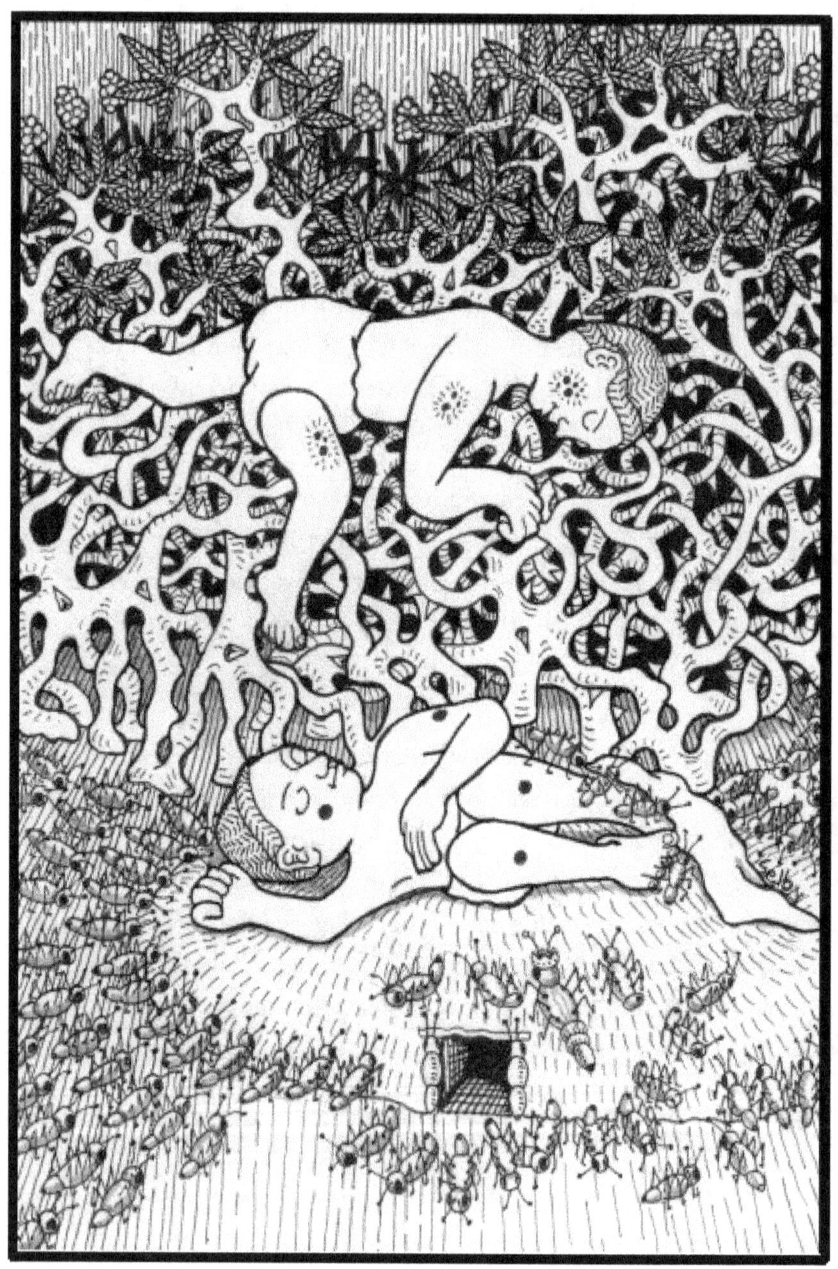

THE TWINS FIRST VISIT

THE TWINS FIRST VISIT

When they arrived at their grandmother's house the twins were crying and upset by the journey.

"Throw them out of here! They are loudmouths!" their grandmother shouted.

One Monkey and One Artisan did not like the new twins because they were very jealous and did not want them around so, while Blood Moon was resting, they put them outside on top of an anthill of 'Fire Ants' where they went right to sleep. When the brothers saw that the ants were happy with the babies they picked them up and threw them in a nearby brambles patch but the babies went straight back to sleep.

Now, Blood Moon could see how they felt so she stayed with her children in the caves in the mountains for many years. When the boys were old enough to make their way through the forest alone they would sometimes go to their grandmother's house. They always took fresh birds that they shot with their blowguns and often berries and fruit they picked from the bushes and trees in the rainforest. Their grandmother would prepare them for herself and her children but she never offered Hunahpu or Xbalanque anything to eat.

One Monkey and One Artisan often made their half-brothers take on the worst jobs that they could think of. They would always do their best until the family chased them home by saying how useless and hopeless they were.

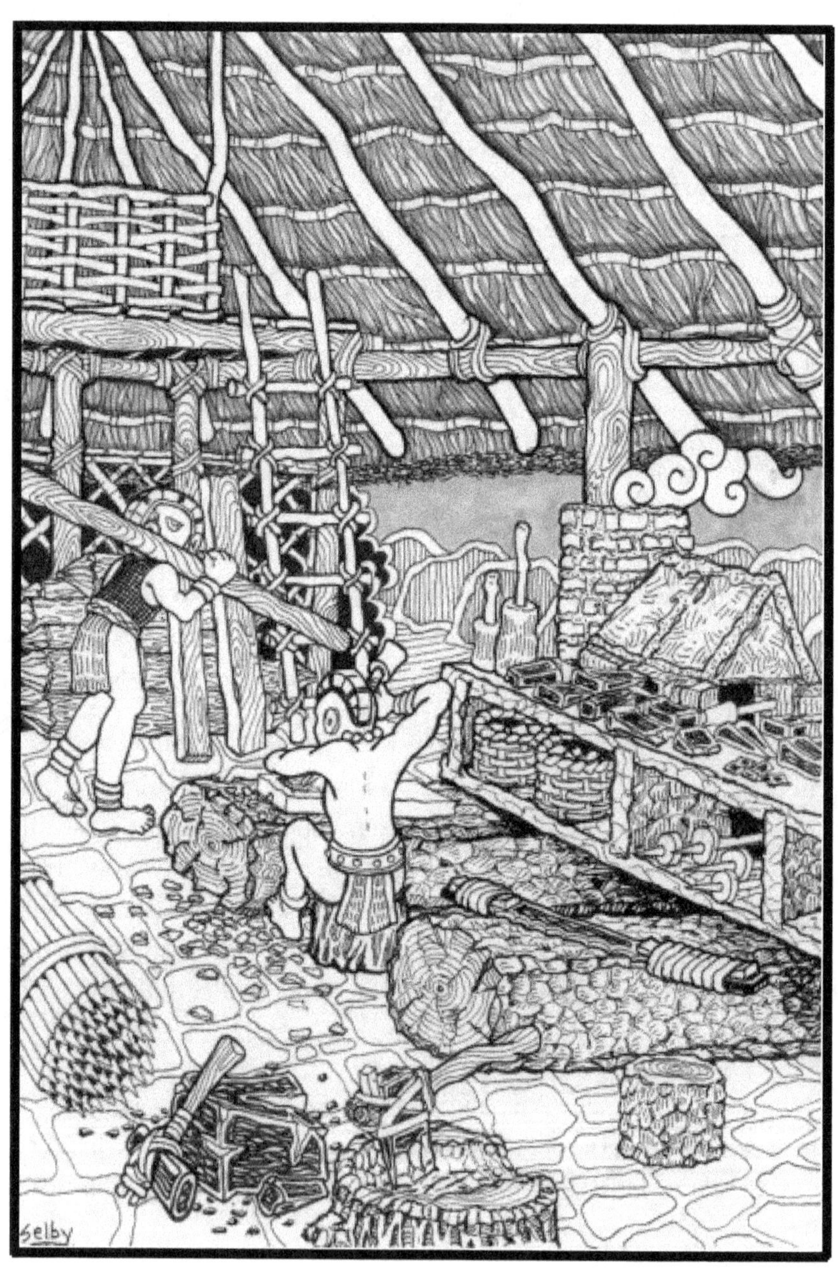

ONE MONKEY AND ONE ARTISAN

ONE MONKEY AND ONE ARTISAN

Since One Monkey and One Artisan were great thinkers, simply geniuses, and did everything well, they understood what their half-brothers were but, they didn't reveal their insight because of their jealousy. The young boys got no love from their brothers or their grandmother. They weren't even given the leftovers from meals they always brought.

It was clear to Hunahpu and Xbalanque where their proper place was in the household but they never got angry or said anything.

Then one day Hunahpu and Xbalanque arrived at the house but they didn't bring any birds. So, their grandmother turned red and shouted, "Now they come here without any birds. Why don't you have any birds? What are we to eat?"

"There are some, our dear grandmother, but our birds just got hung up in the tree and we are too small to climb the tree, our dear grandmother. Can our elder brothers please go with us, to please get the birds down from the tree, dear grandmother."

"Very well we will go with you at dawn," their elder brothers replied

Now they had won the fall of One Monkey and One Artisan. "So be it, since they have cost us great suffering. They wished that we would just die and disappear, just as they wish us to be slaves here. So we shall defeat them. We shall just show them a sign but not hurt them," they each thought.

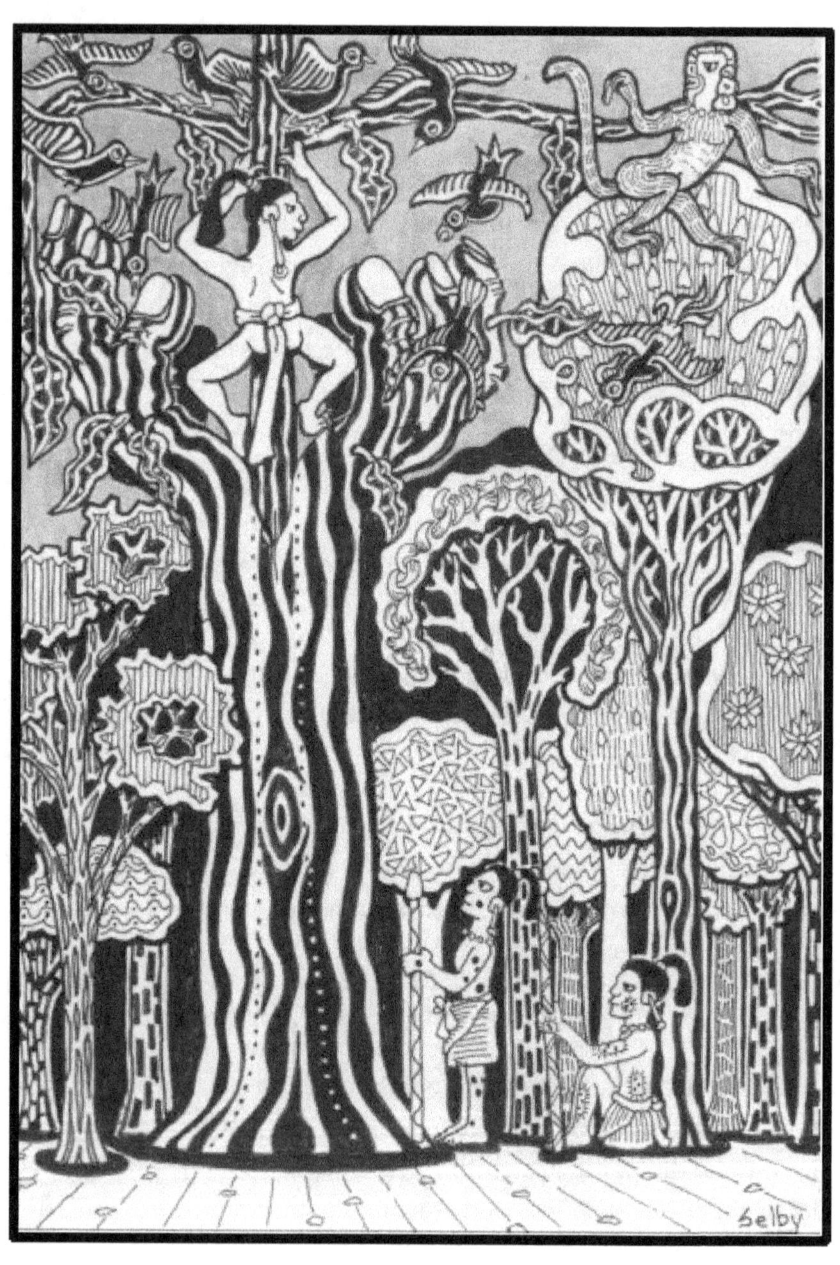

DEFEAT OF ONE MONKEY AND ONE ARTISAN

DEFEAT OF ONE MONKEY AND ONE ARTISAN

The next day, in the big yellow tree, there were many birds. Their older brothers had never seen so many birds in one place but not one bird fell from the tree when they had been shot

"See what we have been saying? Those birds just don't fall. You need to go up the tree and throw them down to us."

The tree would be easy to climb thought the older boys so up they went. Getting to the top was not hard for them but as they started to collect the birds that had been shot the tree got bigger and started to grow taller. The trunk was smooth with no branches and it was getting larger and larger. Almost in the blink of an eye, they could see that they could not get back down.

Hunahpu and Xbalanque could see what was happening so they shouted up to their half-brothers, "Quick! Tie your loincloths around your waist and leave the long part hanging down your back. Then jump to that other tree below you. Hurry!"

But, just as they tied the knot in their loincloths they became monkeys. The loincloths became real tails and in the same instant, they were covered in hair and started making god-awful noises that only monkeys can make.

Hunahpu and Xbalanque continued to try and make them jump to the lower tree but they were having way too much fun as they went through the forest howling and swinging through the branches and vines.

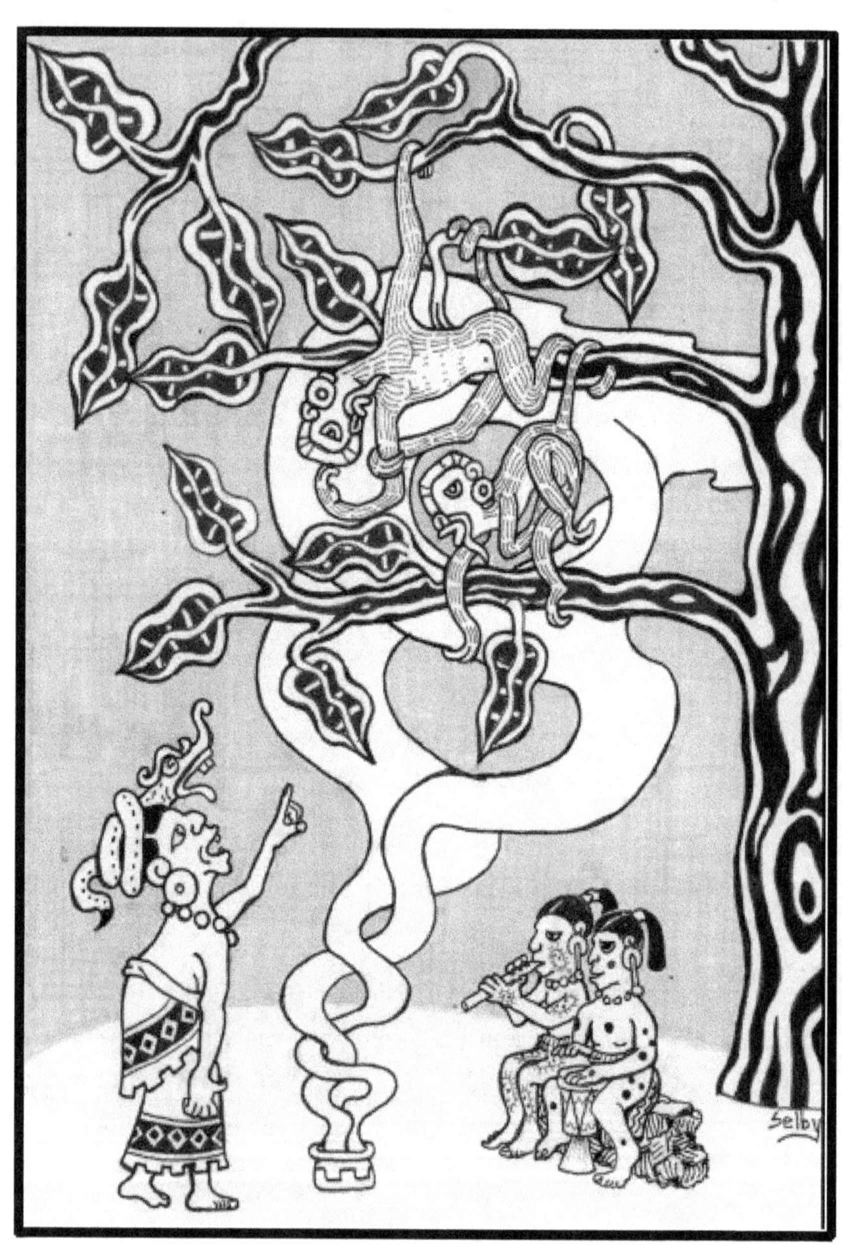

HUNAHPU AND XBALANQUE TELL GRANDMOTHER

HUNAHPU AND XBALANQUE TELL GRANDMOTHER

Now, this is the first time that Hunahpu and Xbalanque discovered their powers. They had not intended to hurt their half-brothers and were sort of sure they could change them back as before but they were a little afraid of what their mother and grandmother would say. When they reached their grandmothers' house they said, "Our dear grandmother, our elder brothers have run off into the woods."

"If you have done something to them, you will have done something very bad to me," she said.

"No grandmother, don't be sad. They have just run off. You can see them when you like. They will come but it will be a bit of a test for you. You must not laugh at them! You must Promise," said the boys.

The boys and their grandmother walked out to the edge of the forest and the boys called them by playing their flute and drums to the tune 'Hunahpu Monkey." And One Monkey and One Artisan came dancing in the trees and up on the roof then over to the big tree in the yard.

Xmucane took one look at them and couldn't stop laughing, so the brothers left right away back to the forest.

"Don't do that our grandmother! We can only call them four times. Please control your laughter even though they are a little different. "We will try again," the boys told their grandmother.

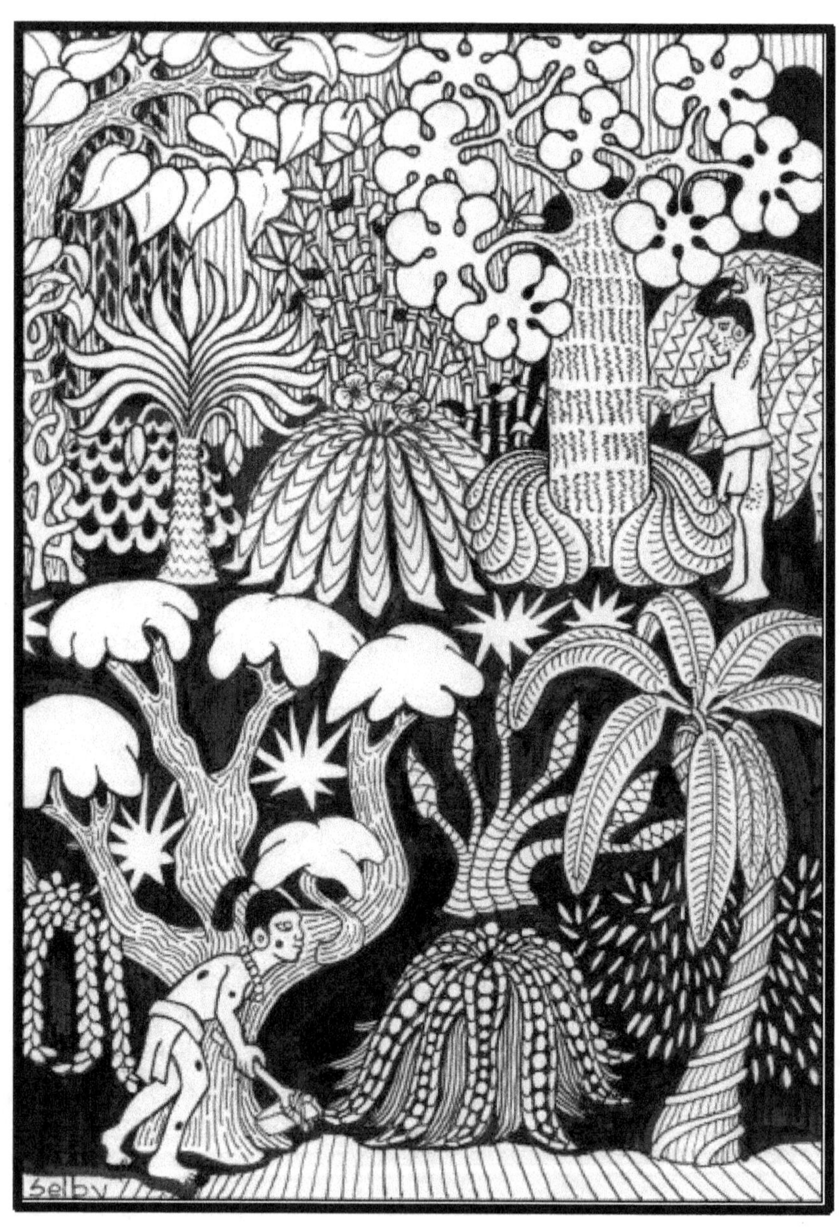

HUNAHPU AND XBALANQUE PLANT

A GARDEN

And, as before, Xmucane just couldn't control herself and laughed and they went back to the forest.

"Please, our dear grandmother, don't laugh at them!"

They tried a third time and it all passed as before but this time Xmucane didn't look at them at first. The boys thought for a moment that they were changing back as they were before but Xmucane opened her eyes and just lost it laughing. This time they went off to the forest never to return.

In ancient times, One Monkey and One Artisan became the gods of the arts and crafts as the first earthlings who made and used artifacts and who themselves became animals.

HUNAHPU AND XBALANQUE PLANT A GARDEN

Soon after their elder brothers were no longer around the twins felt they should look after their mother and grandmother. Not that their elder brothers had done much but perhaps they felt guilty about them running off to the forest. Early one morning the boys collected an ax and a hoe each and with their blowguns on their shoulders they went off to clear a patch of land for their garden. They left the house after arranging for their lunch to be brought to them at midday by their grandmother.

After they found where they thought would be the best place for the garden they went to work clearing it. Well,

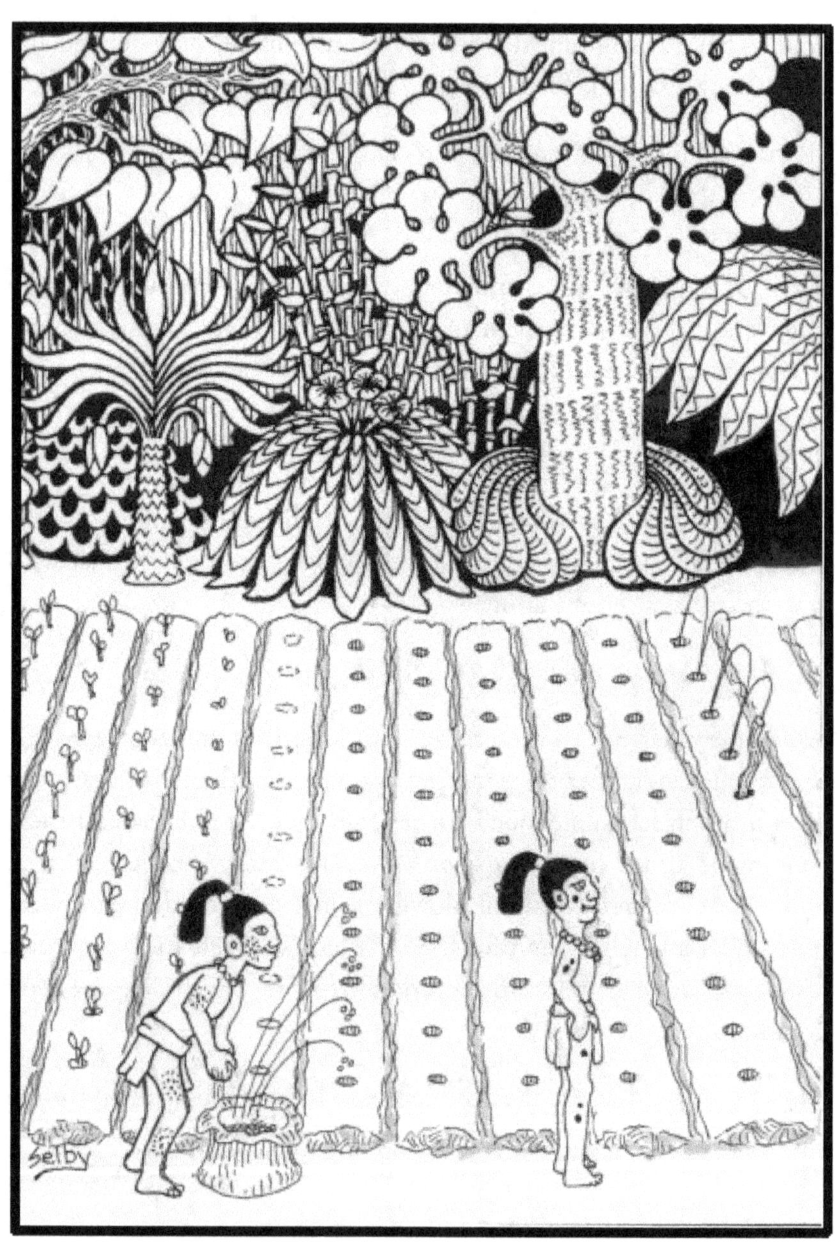

SOWING THE GARDEN

perhaps it is more correct to say that their magic went to work for them. When Hunahpu hit the first tree with his ax, the ax just went about chopping all of the tSOWING THE GARDENrees he wanted to cut down, on its own. While Hunahpu's ax was busy doing this, Xbalanque set his hoe into the ground and the hoe just set about turning over all of the ground for the garden, all on its own.

SOWING THE GARDEN

The boys watched and rested in the shade of a large tree while the ground for the garden was prepared.

When this was done, Hunahpu got out the planting stick and stuck it into the ground where he wanted the first hole for the seed corn. Again the planting stick just hopped down the row that he imagined while Xbalanque opened the seed sack and watched the seeds jump out of the sack, three at a time, and fly to the new hole being made by the planting stick.

All of this was done in a couple of hours so they had plenty of time before Xmucane would bring their lunch. So they decided to do some bird hunting but they thought it better not to show Xmucane what they were doing. They called a 'morning dove' to sing out when their grandmother came with their lunch and when that was arranged, they went to find birds.

As soon as the dove cried out they rushed to the garden to grab their tools while rubbing dirt on their faces and putting sawdust in their hair. After eating and explaining

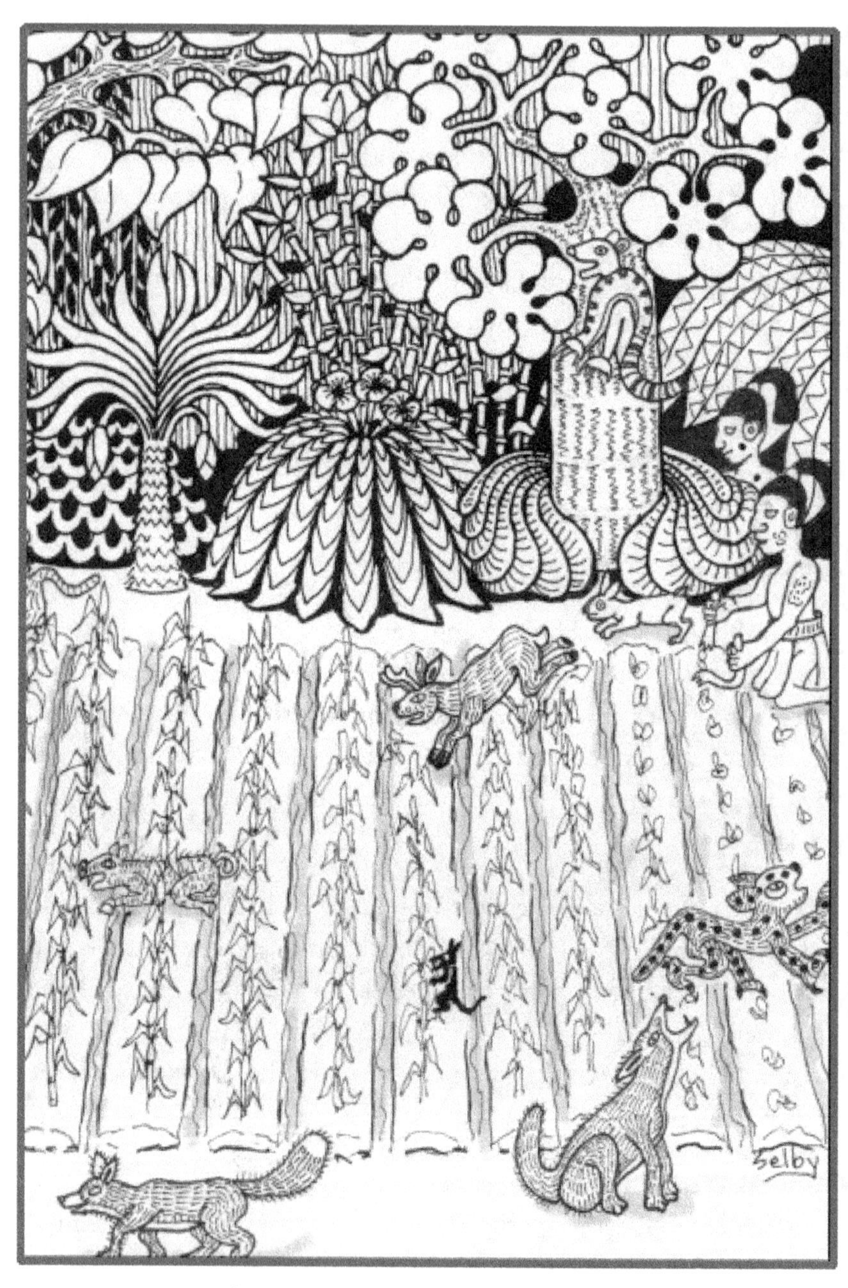

THE GARDEN IS GONE

how tired they were from all their hard work, they walked back to the house with their grandmother.The next morning they rushed to the garden expecting to see great results from their cultivation. Imagine their great surprise to find everything back to its natural order. Every tree, bush, bramble, and weed was put back as it was before they started.

THE GARDEN IS GONE

Not to be defeated they quickly put the garden back in the order they had left it the day before.

"Now we must keep watch to see who is doing this," they decided. "We will have to watch over our garden tonight".

They found cover at the edge of the garden that night and at midnight animals of all types, large and small crept up to the edge of the trees surrounding the garden. All the animals spoke together saying, "Stand up trees, rise bushes, grow weeds and brambles."

At this point, the boys rushed out and tried to grab the animals but the puma and jaguar got away easily. They managed to grab the deer and the rabbit by their tails but they just broke off, which is why they have such short tails to this day. The coati, coyote, fox, and peccary got away but they did manage to get the rat.

The boys were very upset that the animals would do such a thing since they had been their friends until now. So without thinking, they grabbed the rat so hard that its eyes.protruded from its head and they held it over a fire until the hair on its tail burnt away. This, of course, is why the rat looks as it does today.

"I will not die by your hand! Gardening is not your calling but, there is something that is. This is why all of us are here!" screamed the rat.

"Where and what is ours?" asked the boys.

"Will you let me go and give me my morsel of food?" asked the rat.

"We will give you your food, so name it!"

"Very well, it is what your fathers, One Hunahpu and Seven Hunahpu left for you. It is that which Heart of Sky wishes you to have. It is what your grandmother does not want you to know about because this is why your fathers died. The ball gaming equipment which is tied up under the roof of your grandmother's house is for you," the rat explained.

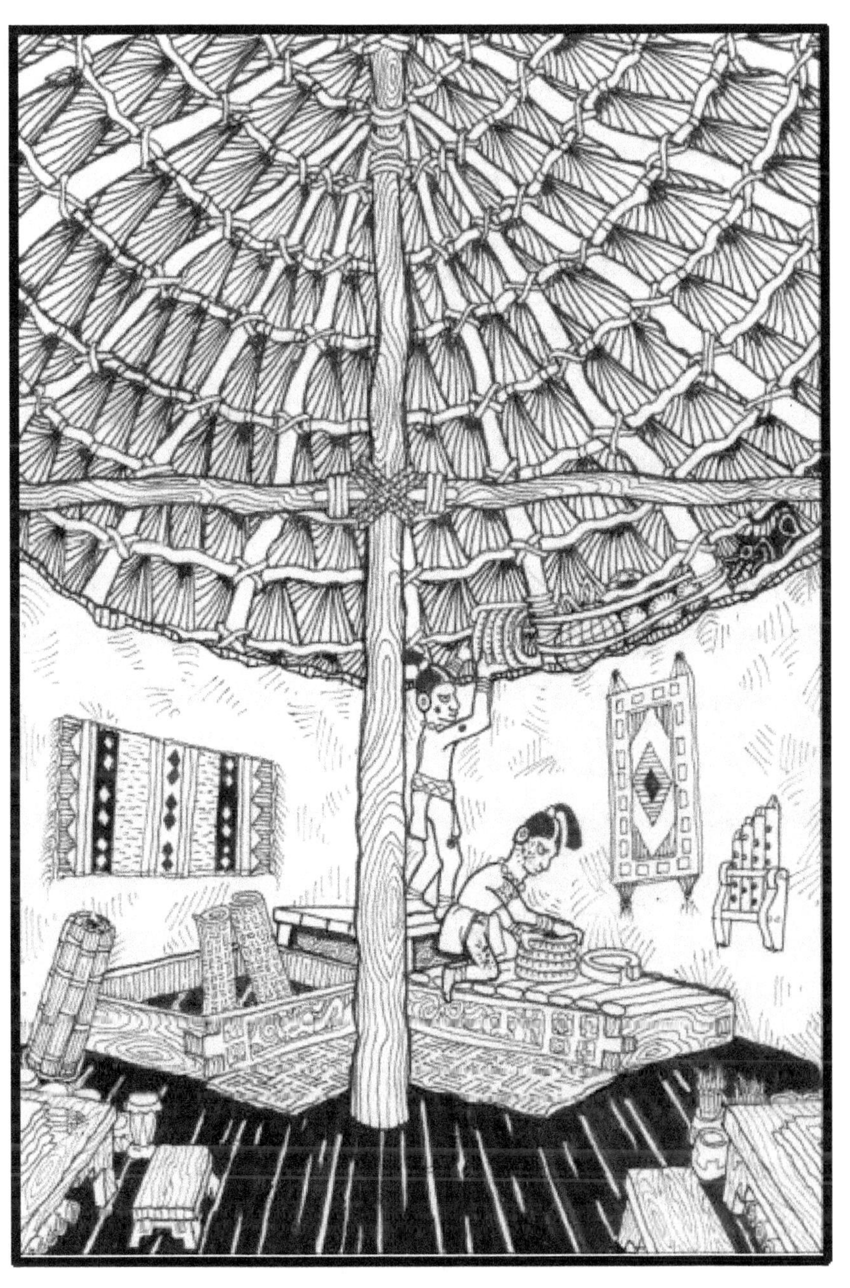

THE BALL GAME EQUIPMENT

THE BALL GAME EQUIPMENT

The boys now understood their destiny and named the future food for the rat and all of his future family, 'corn kernels, squash seeds, chili, beans, palate, cacao, and if your share gets wasted or stored just gnaw away at anything."

The twins made their plans that night and in the morning they smuggled the rat into the house of their grandmother. They explained to their grandmother that they would need water to take to the garden and would she get it for them while they got ready. They had used a mosquito to make a hole in the side of the water jug. When the grandmother didn't return they sent their mother to see what was wrong.

The rat then did its work by gnawing the cords that held the ball game equipment in the rafters. The boys quickly hid the equipment outside where they could get to it without being seen and then went to the spring repaired the jug and carried the water to the house for their mother and grandmother.

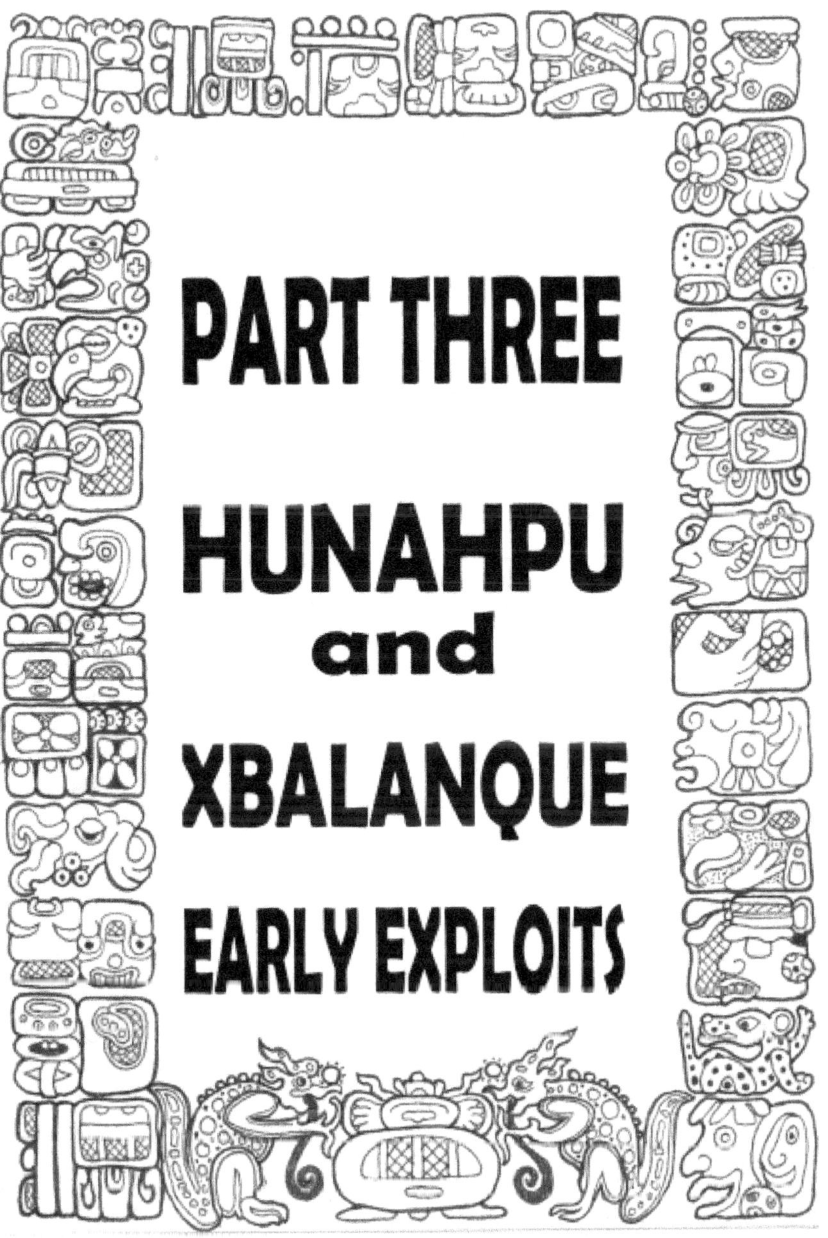
PART THREE

HUNAHPU
and
XBALANQUE

EARLY EXPLOITS

PART THREE

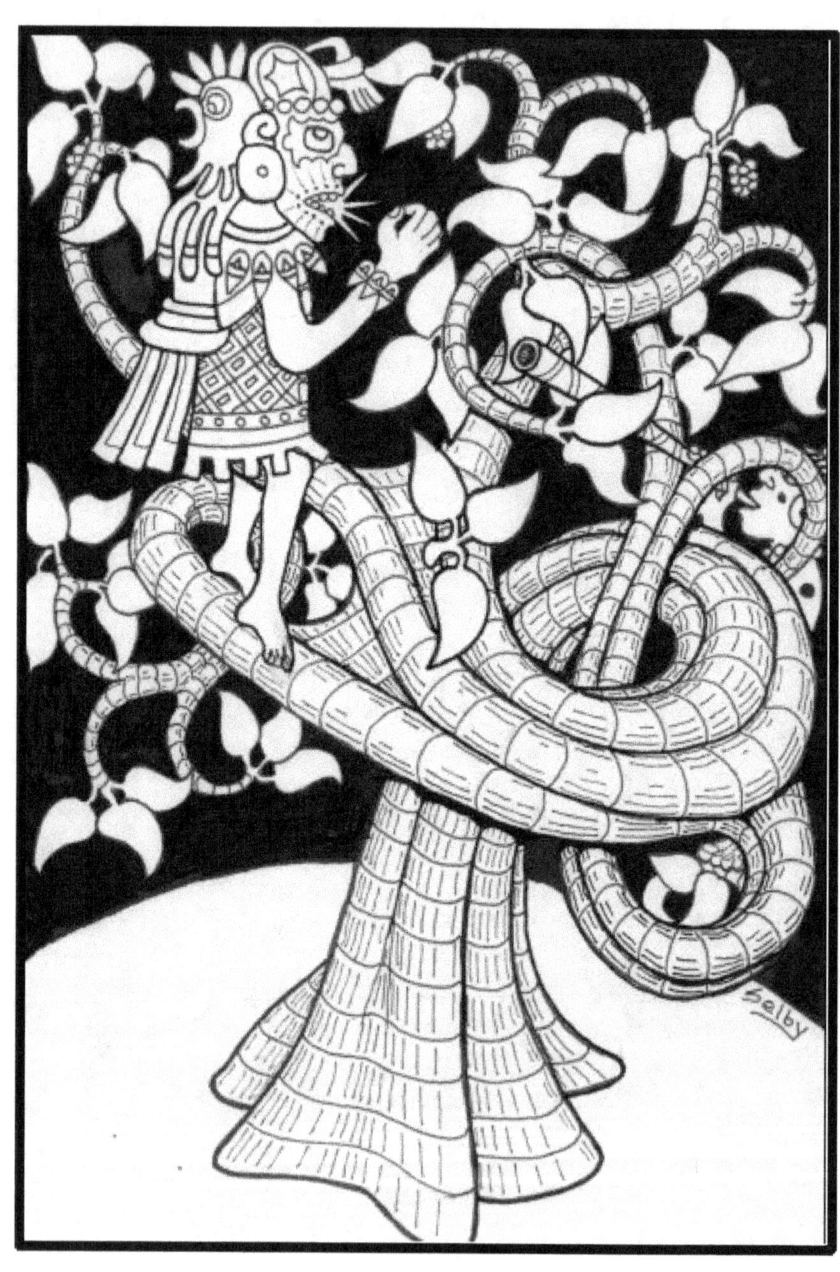

SEVEN MACAW

SEVEN MACAW

The sky is still covered in heavy clouds although the sun and the moon are in the sky. During this time there is one who magnifies himself by saying that he alone is the light of the dawning and higher than the Human Work. He has put metal around his eyes and jewels and turquoise in his teeth that glitter brightly. His nose shines brighter than the moon. He has made wings and sits in the treetops to shine. He calls himself Seven Macaw and puffs himself up and magnifies himself which Heart of Sky finds most exasperating.

Seven Macaw had two sons. The first of which was a giant, huge, and very strong. Who claimed to be the creator of mountains. He has said that he made the mountains named at the dawning as Ixcanul, Macamob, and Huliznab which he said he made in one night.

Seven Macaw's second son was called Earthquake, who claimed he moved mountains small and great. He too was very large and strong,

"I am the Sun," said Seven Macaw. "I am the maker of the earth," said Zipacna. "I bring down mountains," said Earthquake.

SHOOTING OF SEVEN MACAW

There was a tree where Seven Macaw went each day to eat and shine in the light that he thought he had given off. This was where Hunahpu and Xbalanque hid themselves in the branches and the leaves.

As Seven Macaw perched on the top of the tree, shining in the light he was shot by Hunahpu. The blowgun shot got him in the side of his face, breaking his jaw and he fell straight to the ground. Hunahpu quickly dropped to the ground and tried to grab him but Seven Macaw was faster and grabbed Hunahpu's arm twisted and pulled it back, right off of his body. Holding his damaged jaw carefully, Seven Macaw then went home taking Hunahpu's severed arm with him.

When he arrived home his wife, Chimalmat, asked him, "What is that?"

"That is the arm of one of those tricksters! They shot me with a blowgun and tried to kill me but I got the better of one of them and got away with his arm. Now he will try and get it back and I will put an end to him. OH, how this jaw of mine hurts! I must go to bed," he explained.

Hunahpu and Xbalanque wasted no time and invoked a white-haired grandfather and grandmother. They are just bent over old people. The grandfather was named Great White Peccary and the grandmother was known as Great White Coati.

The boys instructed them how to act and sent them ahead telling them to say they had homeless grandchildren on the road following them.

By the time the old ones passed the house of Seven Macaw, he was moaning in the shade of the door. He looked up as the old people were passing and asked where they were going.

"We are just making our living, your lordship," replied the old man.

"Are those your children?" asked Seven Macaw.

Stopping, the old man said, "No your lordship. They are our grandchildren but it is us that take pity on them because they have lost their parents. We must feed them with what little we have, your lordship."

"What is it that you do?" asked Seven Macaw.

"I just pull worms out of teeth and cure eyes. And my wife sets bones, your lordship," replied the old man.

"Then, please cure my teeth, they are loose and my jaw is broken. I can't eat or sleep. Can you fix this?"

"Very well, your lordship. It must be a worm, gnawing at the bone. It is just a matter of taking out your teeth and replacing them, your lordship," said the old man.

"It is not good that my teeth come out because I am a lord and my teeth and eyes are my most important feature."

"You need not worry, your lordship, We will replace them with ground bone and they will appear the same as before," said the grandfather but he only had ground white corn.

"Very well, Just pull them out and take away this pain

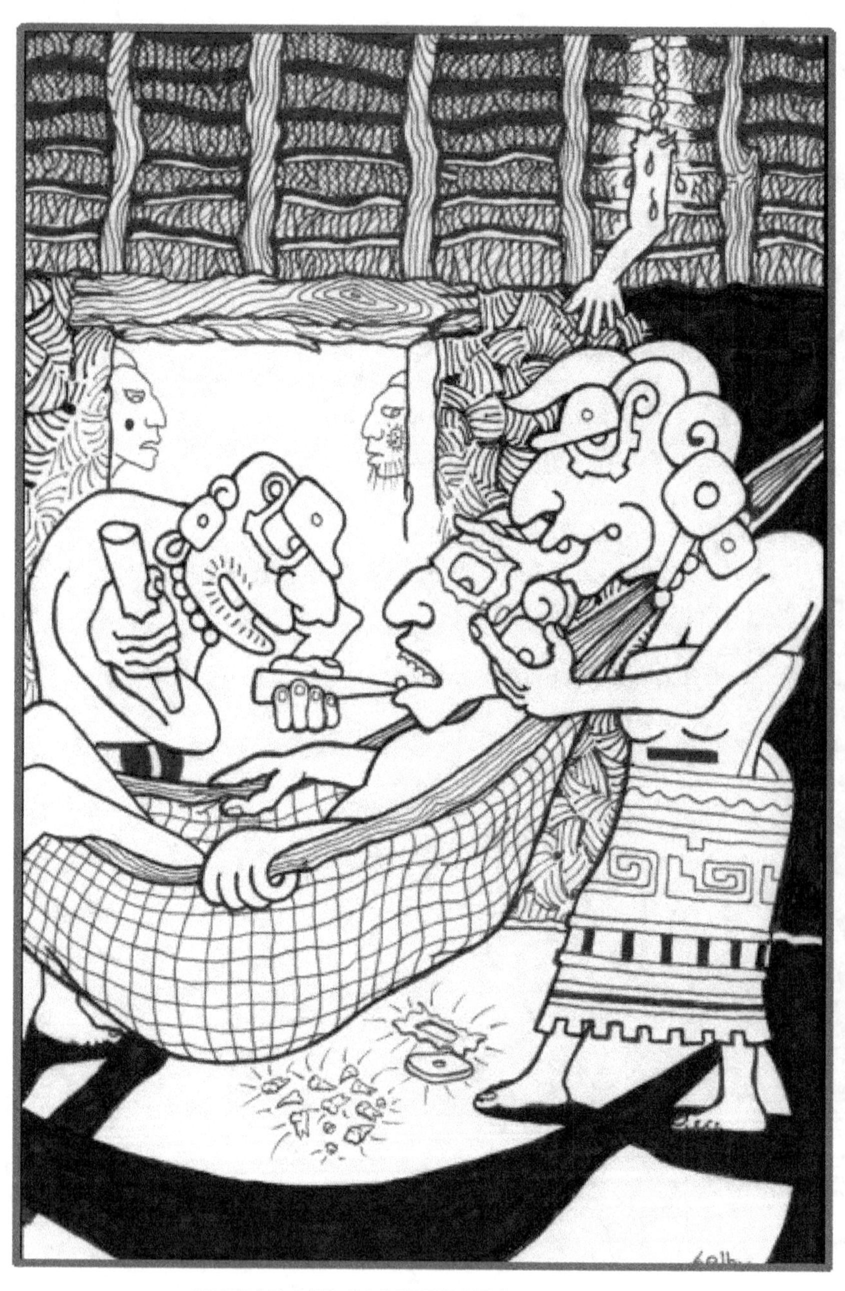

DEFEAT OF SEVEN MACAW

80

The grandfather then set about knocking all of Seven Macaw's teeth out with a stone hammer and chisel taking great care not to damage the jewels that were embedded in his teeth. He then rolled ground corn in a long roll and stuffed it in the empty holes.

The grandmother meanwhile removed the silver frames from his eyes and his gold ear decorations leaving a rather drab Seven Macaw but was careful to collect everything to take with them.

Seven Macaw never recovered from this ordeal. Because he had lost his shine he lost his will and his wife soon followed.

Xbalanque entered the house and retrieved the arm of Hunahpu and the old woman put it back in its place and bound it well, so it would heal.

Just as Heart of Sky had wished for the death of Seven Macaw so they had made it happen.

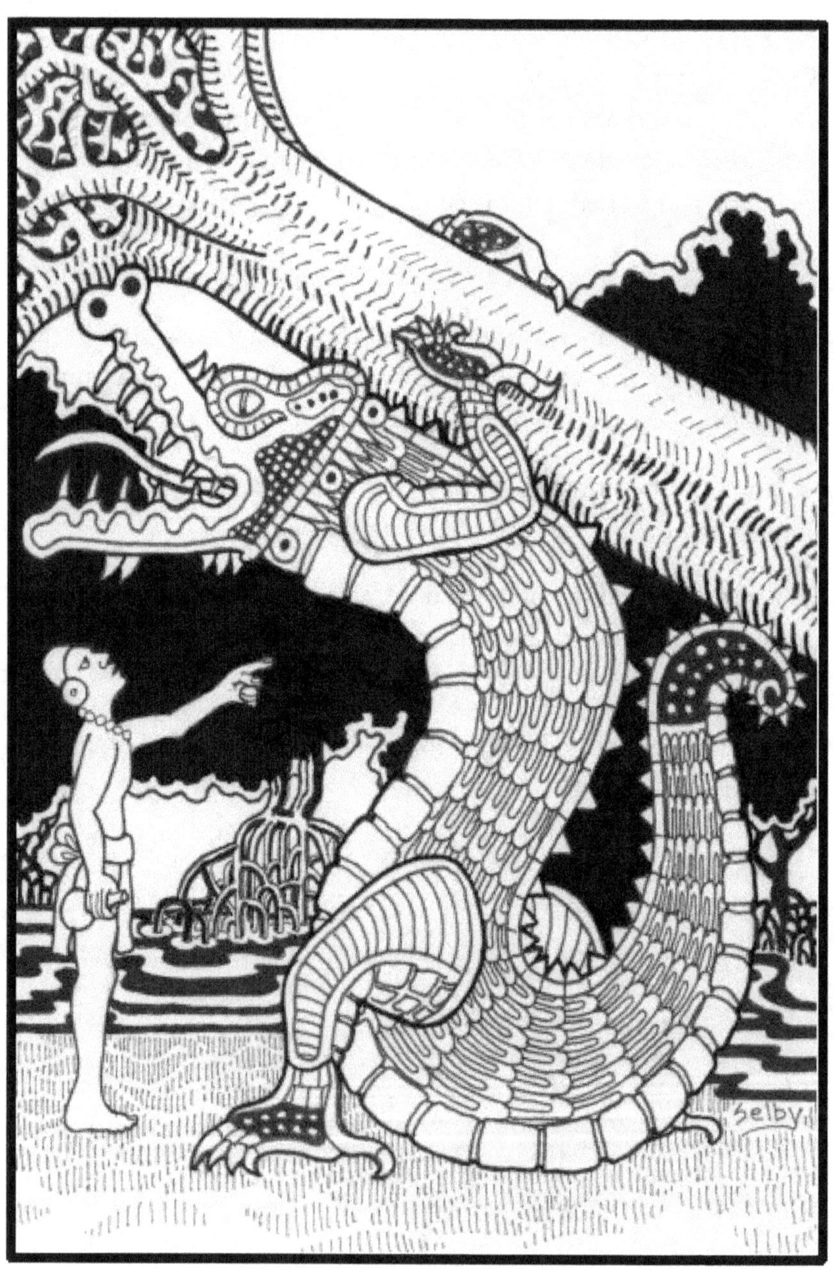

Selby

THE DEEDS OF ZIPACNA

THE DEEDS OF ZIPACNA

"I am the maker of mountains," said Zipacna.

Zipacna was the first son of Seven Macaw and Chimalmat during the dawning of the earth. He was depicted as a caiman in classical times but should not be confused with Heart of Sky who could also manifest himself as a caiman but always had the headdress which contained a hurricane. Although Zipacna may have seen himself as the equal to Heart of Sky who is often called Hurakan, he was not. Zipacna was very big and strong and very prone to thinking he was better than he was.

Zipacna lived near a group of boys (400 it is said) that found much pleasure in brewing alcoholic drinks. As the story opens the 400 boys are building a new place to live and play in but they find Zipacna not a neighbor of choice and plan how to kill him.

The plan is simple, they dig a hole for a huge center post to hold up the new roof. They cut down a large tree and ask Zipacna to move it to the hole, ask him to go down the hole and dig it a bit deeper, and then drop the tree down the hole killing him.

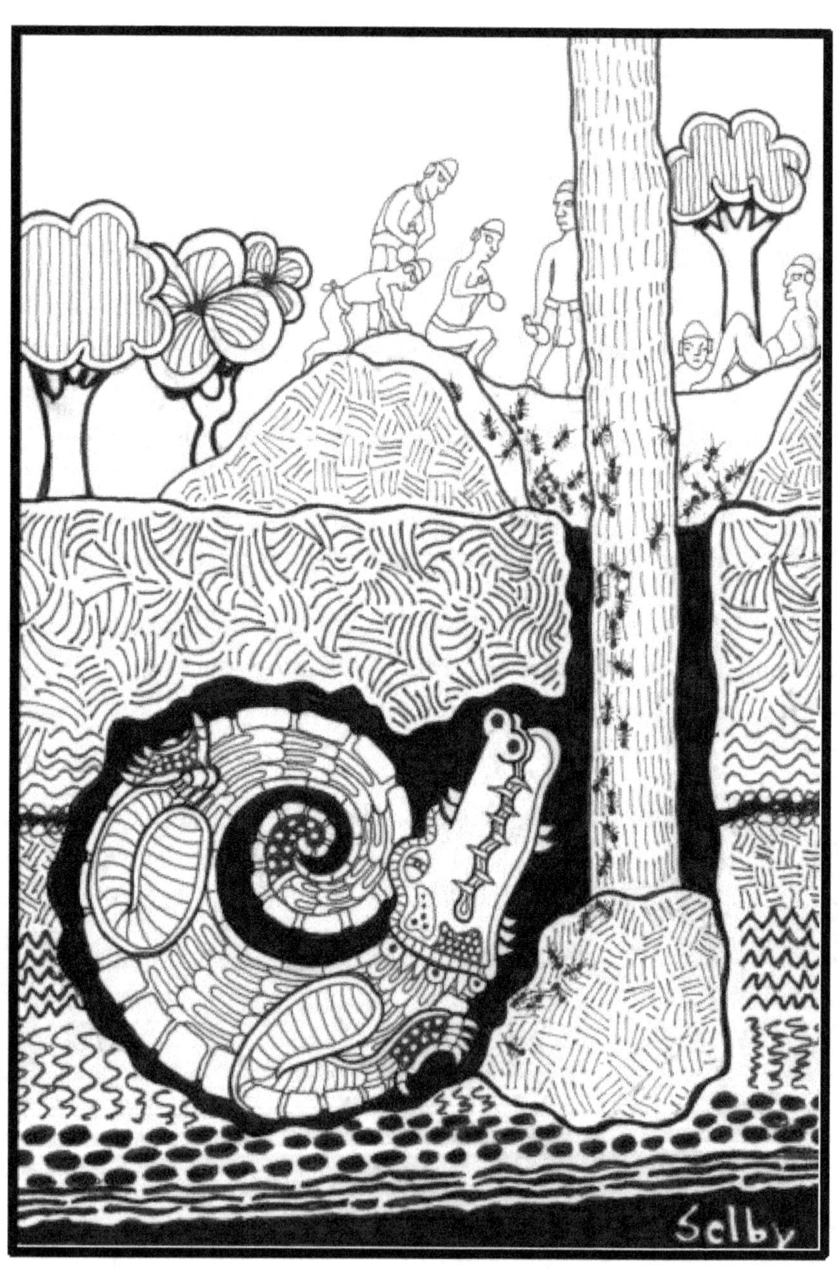

ZIPACNA ESCAPES

ZIPACNA ESCAPES

Alcohol does not always improve thinking. Zipacna manages to move the huge tree to the hole. He then goes down the hole to dig it deeper but to make room for his huge body he dug a cave next to the bottom of the hole so he can work better.

Down comes the tree and Zipacna is not hurt. The boys test the assassination by dropping a nest of ants down the hole and waiting to see if the ants bring up any bits or pieces.

Zipacna may not be the smartest but when the ants come down the hole he figures it out and pulls out some hairs bites off a bit of his fingernails and feeds them to the ants. The ants climb out of the hole carrying what the 400 boys think is the last of them and they go off in good cheer to get drunk. Bad idea!.

This gives Zipacna time to dig himself out of the hole and while the 400 boys are sleeping it off, he brings their house down on top of them, killing them all.

Now, who has won? Well, the 400 boys become the constellation we call the Pleiades and many of the other stars while Zipacna is brought to the attention of Hunahpu and Xbalanque by Heart of Sky.

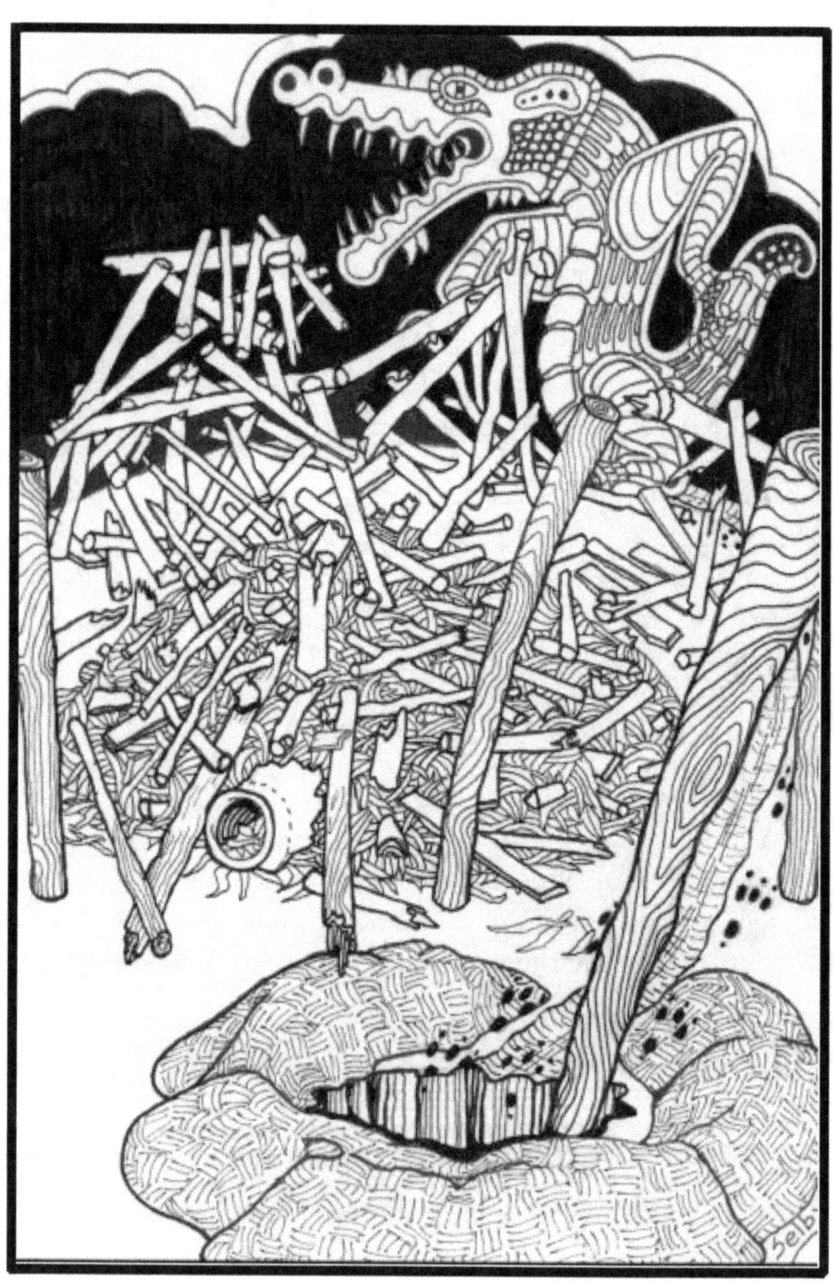

DEFEAT OF ZIPACNA

DEFEAT OF ZIPACNA

Zipacna is big and must spend his days looking for fish and crabs around the waters where he lives and I suppose lifting mountains as he has said.

Hunahpu and Xbalanque picked bromeliads that grow in the trees of the tropical forest and used them as claws and legs for a huge crab that they made The body of the crab was a large flagstone that clattered when it was moved which they colored from berry juice and sap. They then found a large hole under a rock overhang at the base of the mountain named Meauan. Here they placed the crab so that Zipacna would have to crawl under the overhanging stone to get to it. Only a little room for such a large person. They then set off to find him.

When they found Zipacna at the water's edge as they expected, they asked him, "What are you doing?"

"Just hunting my food, crab, and fish but, there aren't any around here," he told them.

"Oh, there is a big crab down in the valley. We tried to catch her but we just got bitten and gave up. You could get her if she hasn't gone," the boys told him.

"We have to go hunt birds but, if you just follow the river to the base of the mountain until you get to the overhanging rock, she is in there they told Zipacna.

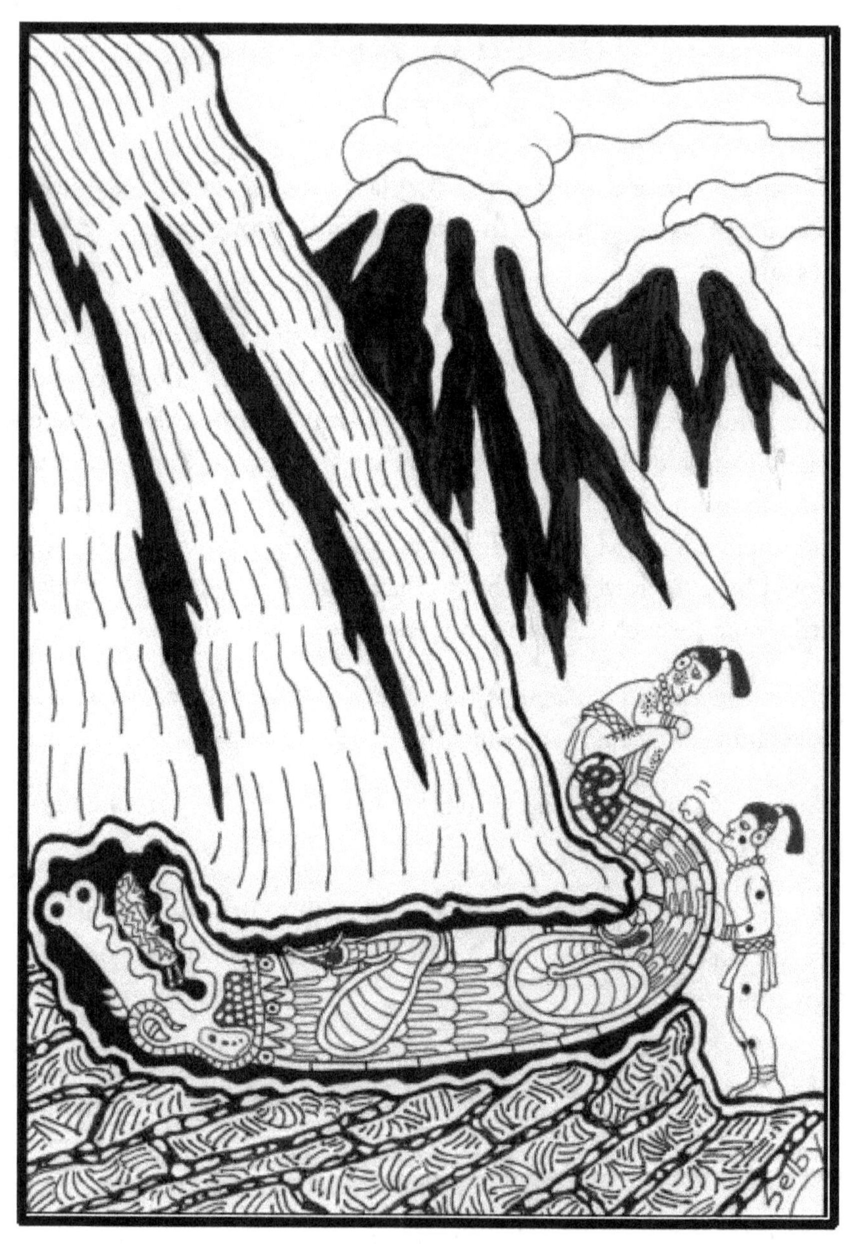

ZIPACNA TURNS TO STONE

"But can't you just take pity on me and show me where to look? I know that there are a lot of birds in that area. Well, sure! We will show you," the boys answered.

On the way down to the river the boys pointed out that they had entered face down but couldn't move enough to catch the crab. "We think you could do it if you entered on your back. That way you could move your arms better."

They arrived at the bottom of the canyon and could see the crab on her side in her bright red shell. In his hurry, Zipacna crawled in face down but the crab got on top of him and he had to back out.

"You can't reach her?" the boys asked.

"Yes, but she got on top of me and I just barely missed her. So I'm going back in on my back. That should work better," he said.

After which he entered on his back with the mountain resting on his chest. He entered all the way, but he couldn't turn over there, so he slowly turned to stone. He who said he was "the maker of mountains" slowly became part of the great mountain, Meauan.

The twins had defeated Zipacna as Heart of Sky had wished.

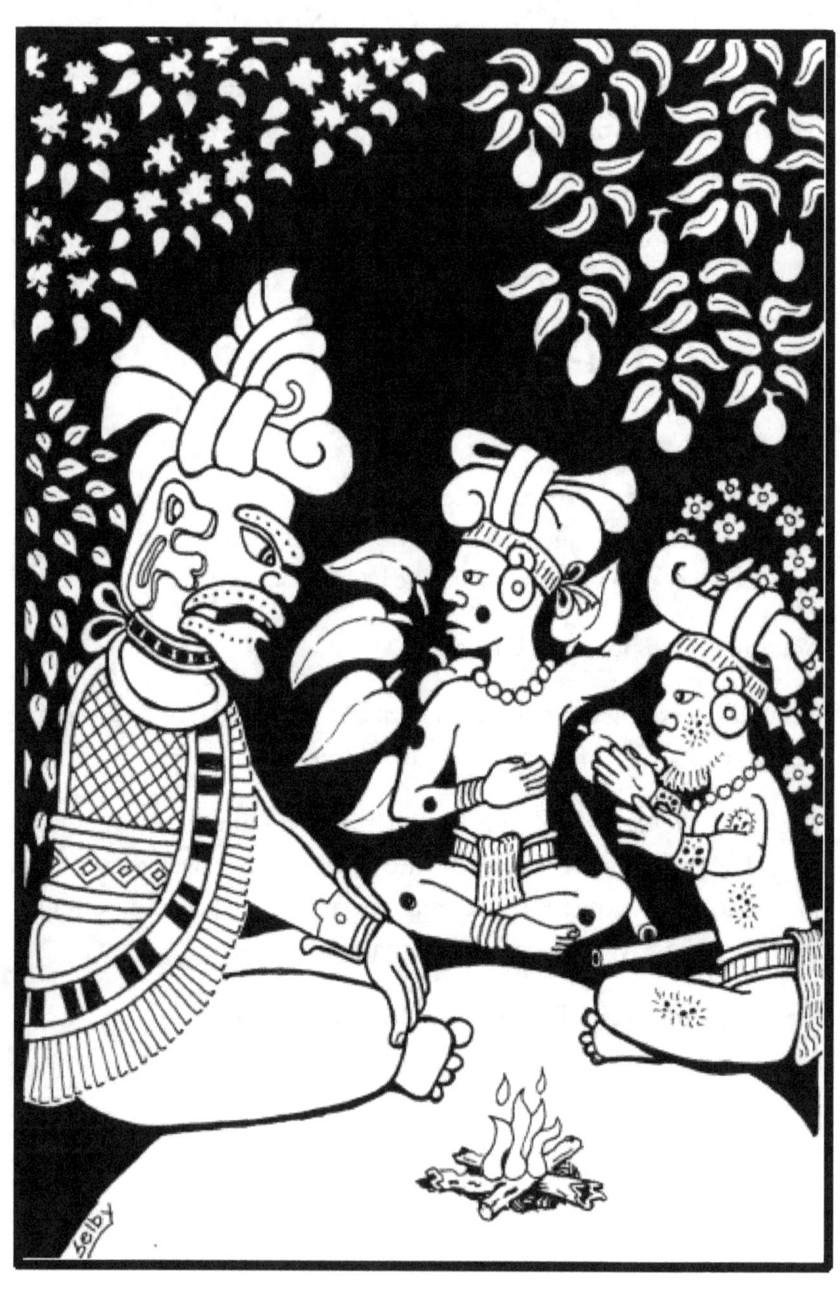

THE TWINS ENCOUNTER EARTHQUAKE

THE TWINS ENCOUNTER EARTHQUAKE

"I am the breaker of mountains great and small," said Earthquake

Now this Earthquake guy was much like his brother, big, strong, and had nothing much to do so he promoted himself as being able to bring down mountains which didn't sit well with the guys that made all the mountains a while back. Heart of Sky talked with Hunahpu and Xbalanque and suggested they take care of the great Earthquake. This is how it went.

One day Earthquake just happened to run across the two boys although it would be better to call them two young men now. They inquired where he was going and Earthquake said, "I'm not going anywhere. I just spend my days breaking up mountains and turning them into sand. What is the point of having so many hills to go over?

He then asked the twins, "Where are you boys from? I haven't seen you before. What are your names?

"We don't have names, we are just orphans and we hunt and trap in the mountains for our food. We have just come down because we were afraid," the twins told him.

"What were you afraid of?" asked Earthquake.

"We saw a mountain that was just growing on its own! It was higher than the rest and we could see that it was getting bigger every day. It was just swelling," they said.

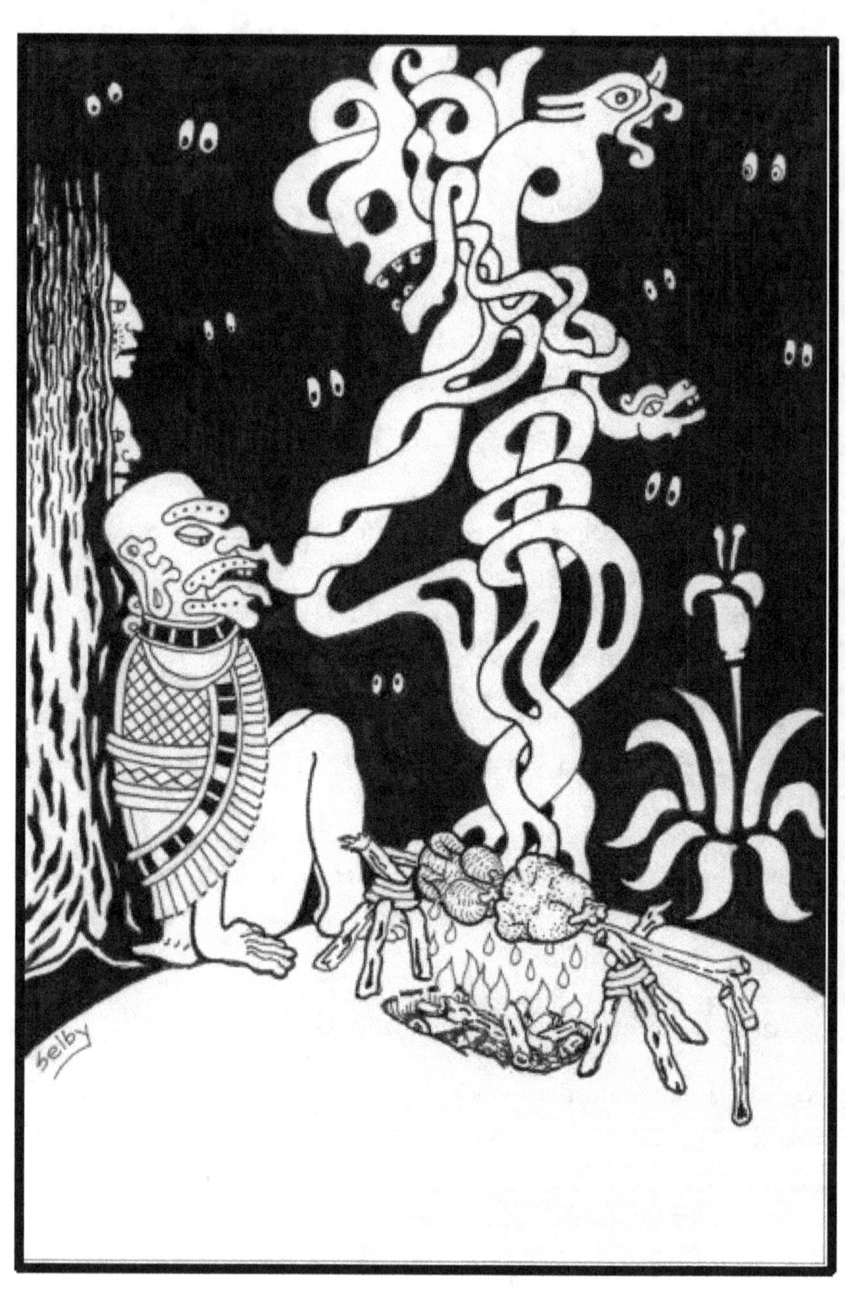

THE DEFEAT OF EARTHQUAKE

THE DEFEAT OF EARTHQUAKE

"This can't be true what you say. I have never seen a mountain like that around here," he said.

"It is not here, it is in the east a couple of days from here. Didn't you tell us you took down mountains like this," said Hunahpu.

"I sure did. Just show me the way and you will see for yourselves. There isn't any mountain I can't knock down!" said Earthquake.

So the boys lead the way to the east. They insisted that Earthquake walked between them telling him that they needed room to swing their blowguns if they saw any birds on the trip and they shot two large birds that first day. Earthquake couldn't get over how they could shoot the birds without an earthen pellet in their guns. They just killed them with air.

Before the night came on they stopped and started a fire by spinning a wooden drill and cleaning the birds in the stream. The bird for Earthquake was rubbed down with white clay and set to one side.

"This is the one that we give him. When he smells these birds he will become very hungry. In earth, we must cock it and in the earth must be his grave. This must happen before the sowing and the dawning of human life can begin. As the heart of Earthquake will desire a bit of flesh so will the human heart desire a bit of meat."

Then they cooked the birds until they were brown, dripping with fat, and giving off a wonderful aroma. It just

had an overwhelming fragrant aroma. The next day as they walked Earthquake lost his great strength and fell by the roadside where they buried him, in the Earth.

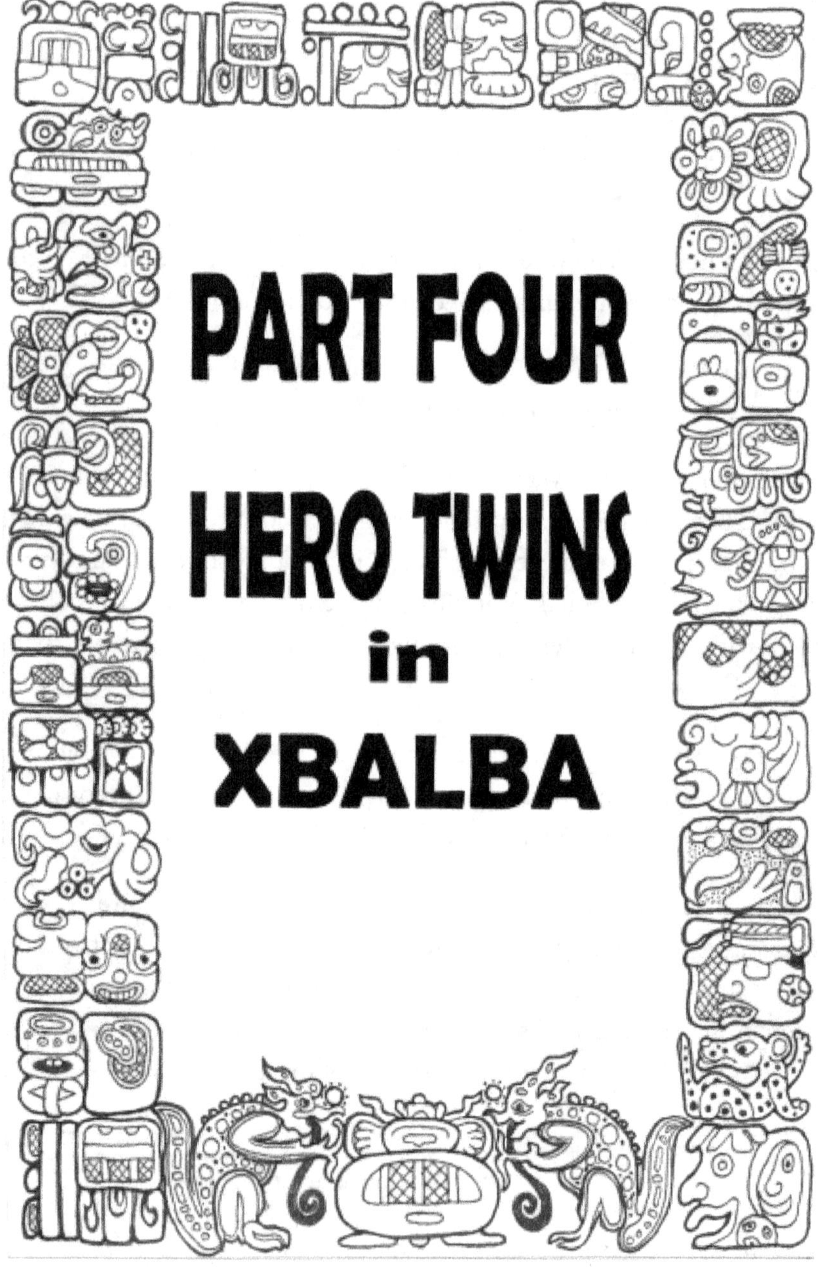

PART FOUR

HERO TWINS
in
XBALBA

PART FOUR

THE SUMMONS TO XIBALBA

Hunahpu and Xbalanque are older now and much more aware of their powers. Some time has passed and they have lived normal lives hunting, maintaining a working garden, and playing ball. They understand their destiny and only wait for their summons to Xibalba to fulfill it. It is their exploits there that will give them eternity as the Maya "Hero Twins".

The making and awakening of humans has yet to come. The full light of the sun and moon has yet to be seen. Xibalba is much the same with the lords having little to occupy them.

Then one day Xbalanque and Hunahpu are playing ball as they so often did, when the lords One and Seven Death, decide that there is too much noise coming from the ball game court again but this time they don't send their normal messagers, the owls. They send instead, a mire louse, and to Xmucane, not directly to the offenders. Xbalanque and Hunahpu. An obvious insult. It was almost as if they didn't want to summon the twins at all.

The grandmother is very upset that this should be happening again and wants nothing to do with it and sends the poor little louse down the road to the ball court on its own.

After not getting very far the louse meets a toad, named Tamazul who listens and then swallows the louse in the hope of getting it to the ball court quickly.

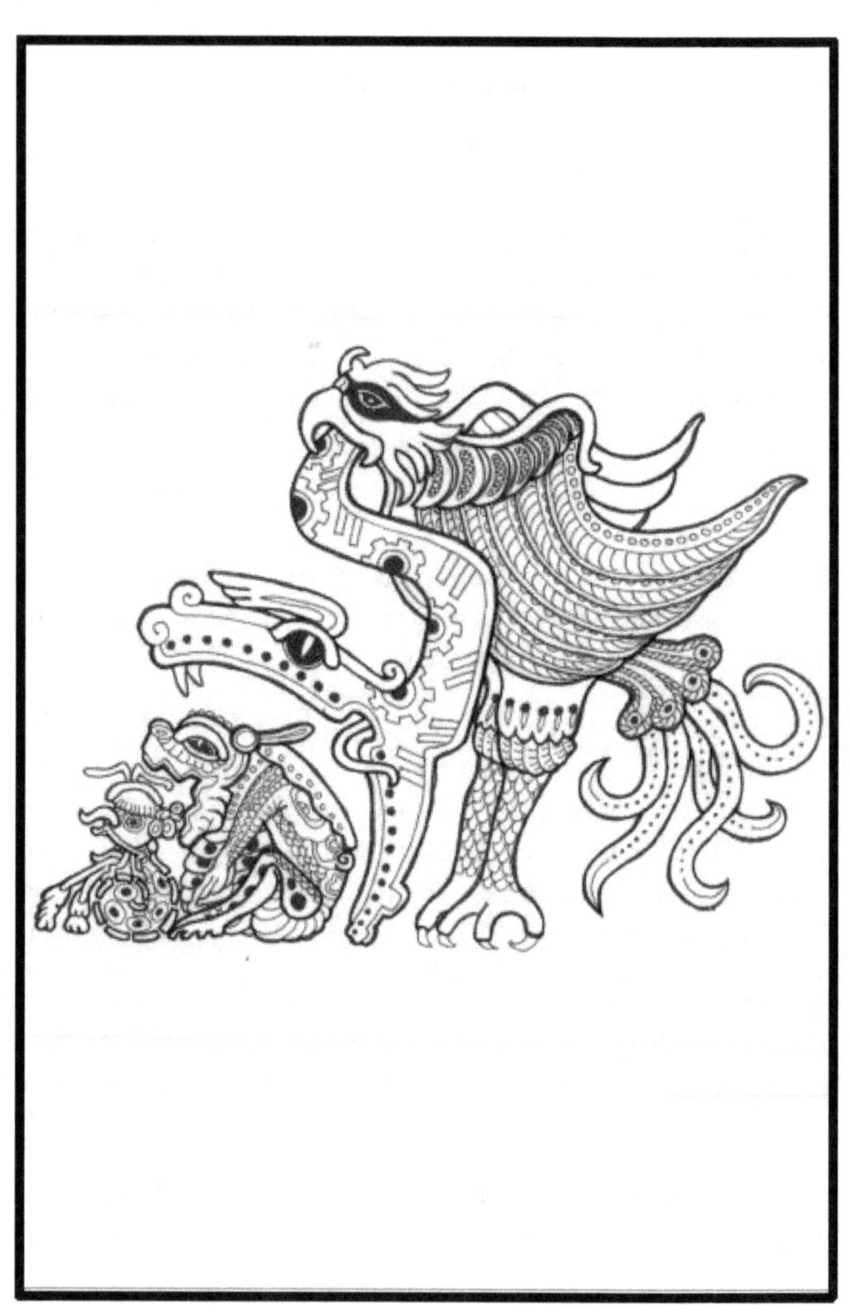

THE SUMMONS TO XIBALBA

The big fat toad doesn't make much headway when they meet a serpent named Zaquicaz. The toad explains

that it has a message in its gut that needs to be given to the twins at the ball court and they then get swallowed.

Next is a falcon who swallows the serpent but when it gets to the ball court he is shot in the eye by the twins. After the twins get the full story they award everyone with their main food in the future, the toad getting the louse, the serpent getting the toad, and so on. The twins then have to fix the eye of the falcon before it will give up what it has swallowed. The falcon gets a new name, "laughing falcon" because of the black patch of rubber they put around his eye.

Xbalanque and Hunahpu go back to their grandmother's house where they get the whole story. "They have seven days to check in to Xibalba and they must bring all of their gaming equipment with them."

The twins then give their grandmother instructions, they each planted corn seeds in the center of the house and when the plants die they may have to die as well, but the plants will regrow and she will then know that they are alive again. So there in the middle of the dry house, they left a sign. They then gathered what they needed and left.

THEIR JOURNEY TO XIBALBA

They quickly descended the steep steps of the cliff face and through the change of canyons. They passed through many "Throng" birds and crossed the River of Pus and the River of Blood using their blow guns to walk over. These were just traps for those who didn't know the way.

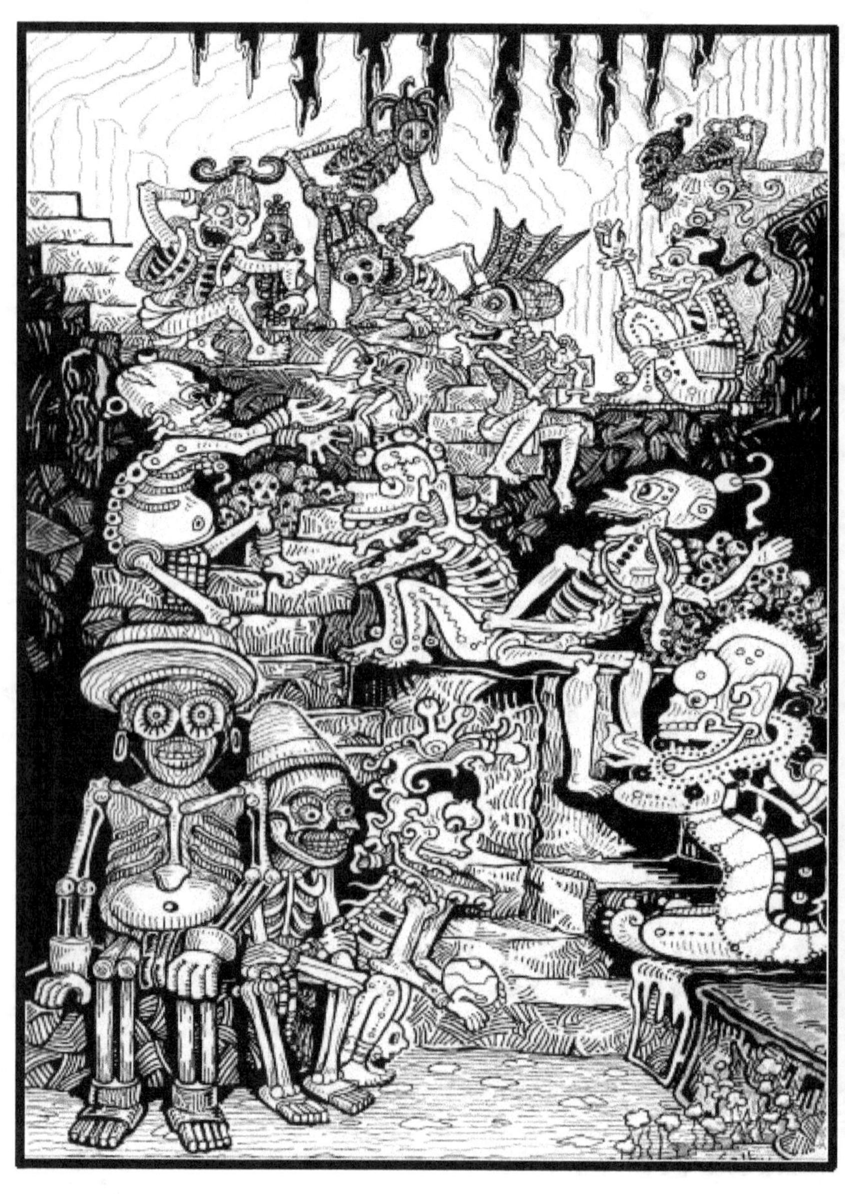

XBALANQUE AND HUNAHPU ENTER XIBALBA

Next, they reach the crossroads but know that it is the Black Road that goes to Xibaba, not the white, red or green roads. Here they called forth a mosquito to go before them as a spy. His reward was the future blood of travelers.

XBALANQUE AND HUNAHPU ENTER XIBALBA

The mosquito entered the council chambers of the lords of Xibalba unnoticed and found the first two seated. He bit them but got no reaction, but knew that these would be the manikins or wood carvings, so he moved on. He bit the next in line and learned this one was alive and kicking and pretty fast with the left hand. He had to be careful with these guys! He also heard the next in line say, "What is it One Death?" He moved on coming in high.

"Yeow!" someone says.

"What is it, Seven Death?" said the one just above. In this way, the mosquito worked his way through the council chamber learning the names and order in which the Lords of Xibalba are sitting.

This was hard work because these guys didn't have much in the way of flesh on their bones. In some cases, he had to take a couple of shots to find any flesh at all. But after he had learned the names of everyone in the chamber he headed for the entrance as fast as he could, which was not easy with all those rocky things hanging from the ceiling.

Once outside he found Xbalanque and Hunahpu close by and gave them the name of each lord of Xibalba and where he was seated. He didn't miss any of them. This was all very strange you see because Xbalanque made the mosquito from a hair he plucked from his nose.

The twins walked straight into the caves of Xibalba, they didn't bother to call out and walked past the two manikins right up to one Death saying;

"Good Day One Death"

"Good Day Seven Death

"Good Day Scab Stripper"

"Good Day Blood Gatherer"

"Good Day Demon of Pus"

"Good Day Demon of Jaundice" "

"Good Day Bone Scepter"

"Good Day Skull Scepter"

"Good Day Wing"

"Good Day Packstrap"

"Good Day Bloody Teeth"

"Good Day BloodyClaws"

They named all of those in the council correctly and in order. No name is missed or incorrect. This was required of them. When told to sit on the hot stone bench they said, "No!" that's for cooking, that's not us. Just one more test by the lords.

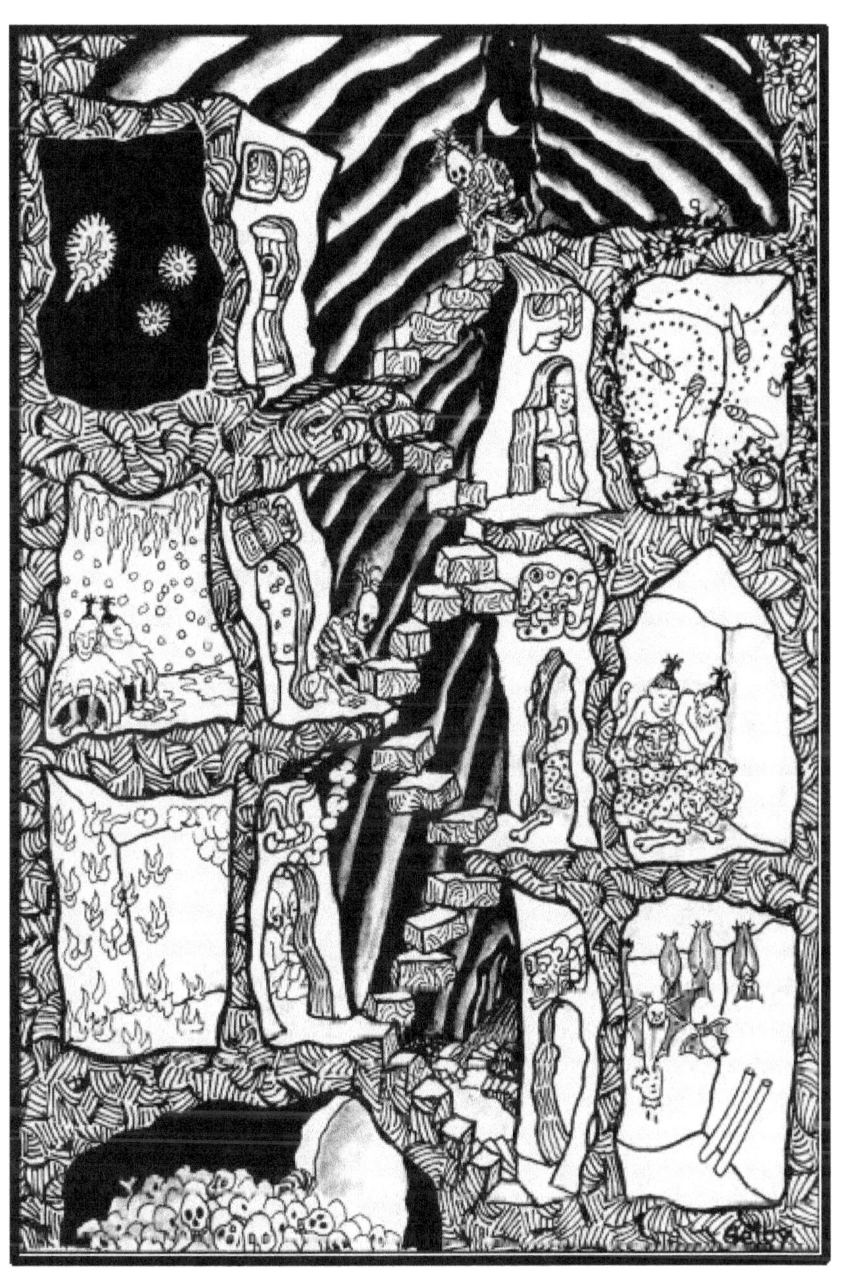

THE TWINS FIRST NIGHT IN XIBALBA

THE FIRST NIGHT IN XIBALBA

Next, they were led to Dark House. This was just the first test of Xibalba and it was very dark as one went in they were given one pine torch and one cigar each and told that they must return them in the morning. Unused! This was how their father, one and Seven Hunahpu were defeated.

"Very Well," they didn't light the cigars. Xbalanque just pulled a little mucus from his nose and made two fireflies which glowed when they were put in the end of the cigars. Xbalanque had brought a couple of Macaw tail feathers that glowed from the light of the fireflies and stuck them in the end of the pine torch. They slept very well that first night.

In the morning the sentres brought the unused cigars and torch to One and Seven Death. The creatures of the underworld had never seen anyone pass their tests before. Who are these guys and where do they come from was the question in all of their minds. So they all thought playing a ball game, full of traps, would defeat these boys.

"Let's play ball," they told the twins.

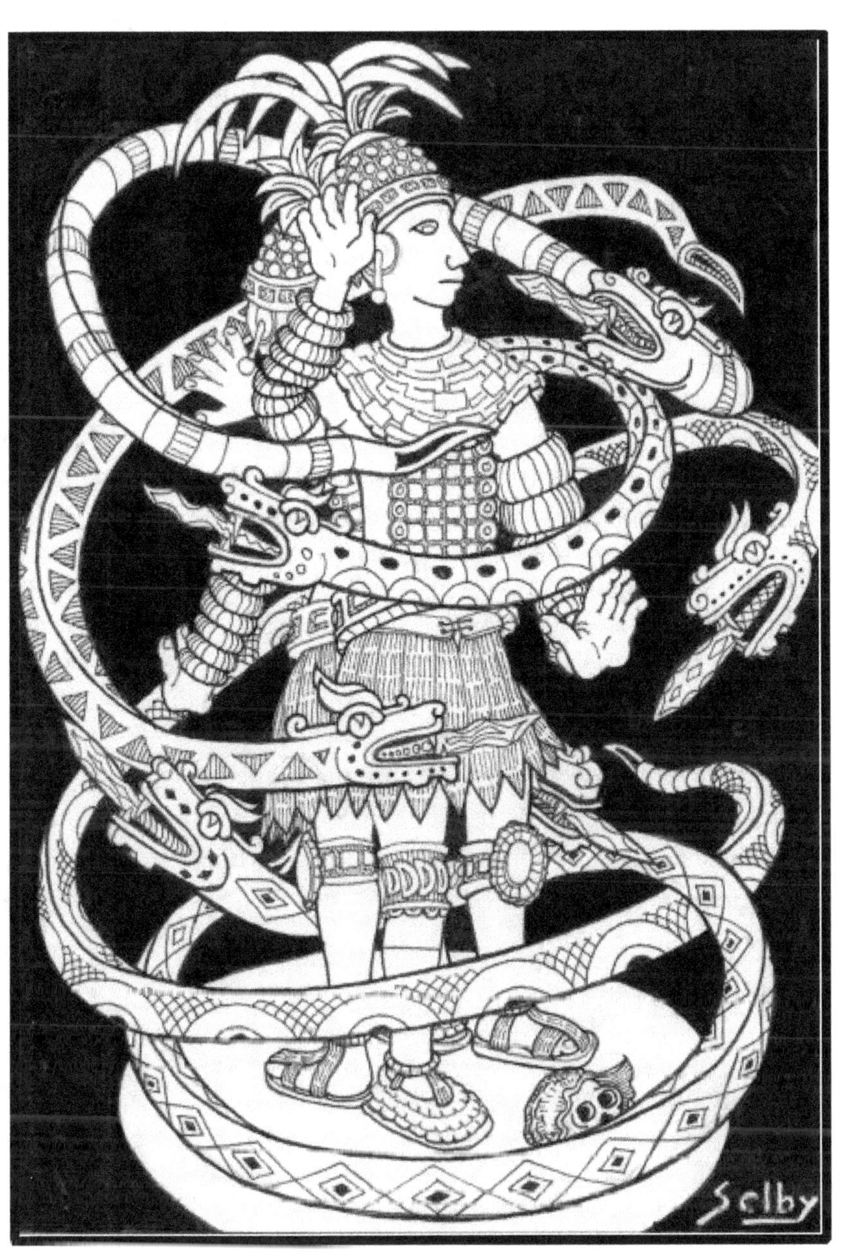

THE TWINS FIRST BALL GAME IN XIBALBA

THE TWINS FIRST BALL GAME IN XIBALBA

The first problem was whose ball should be used. The Xibalban wanted their ball which was nothing but a skull covered in ground bone but the boys knew that it would be a trick but gave in just to get things moving. When the game started the first thing that Xbalanque did was stop the ball with his yoke. While the Xibalban stood watching, White Daggers of Sacrifice, came out from inside the skull and swirled around the twins with such speed they looked like twisting snakes.

The twins stood back to back for a while enjoying the sight, then raised their hands and the knives fell to the ground with a great clatter.

"What is this? You are the ones who sent to us. Why? Only to kill us? If this is the case, we will just leave!" Xbalanque said. This of course was the plan, that the boys should have been defeated by the knives but it didn't work out that way.

So after some talk, it was decided that the rubber ball that the boys brought would be used but if the boys lost the game they would have to fill three bowls of flower petals; one red, one white, and one yellow, and another of whole flowers.

In Xibalba, there is only one place where flowers grew and that was guarded day and night but, the twins agreed to this without question

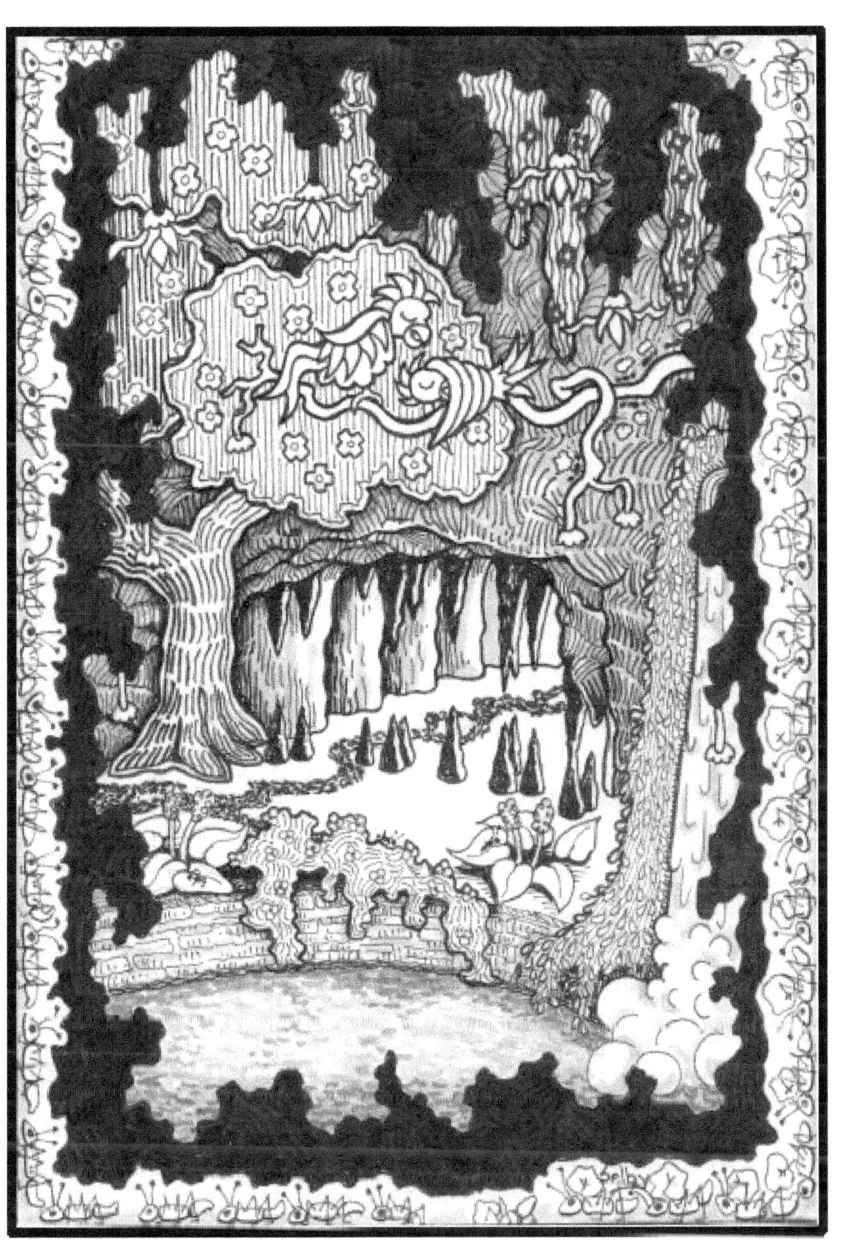

THE SECOND NIGHT IN XIBALBA RAZOR HOUSE

Finally, the game started and the boys were stronger and had much more experience but they chose to lose. This win pleased the Xibalbans and they had visions of defeating

the twins since they had only overnight to find and collect the flowers or would be killed in the house of knives where they had to spend the night.

THE SECOND NIGHT IN XIBALBA RAZOR HOUSE

In this test knives just fly all over the place. Not just one or two but many and a quick death is expected but, it didn't happen that way. The twins spoke to the knives telling them that, "The flesh of all animals would be theirs in the future." All of the knives stopped and put their points in the ground for that night.

Next, they summoned all of the Ants, saying,

"Cutting ants, conquering ants, parasol ants come round,

All of you, fetch all flowers found,

Red, white, yellow petals and one whole, impound

Flowers in bloom, prizes for the blooming lords."

The Whippoorwills of Xibalba were guarding the garden that night but noticed nothing from their perch high in the trees while all night long lines of countless ants picked the flowers and trees clean.

First thing in the morning the lords rush to see the boys' bodies only to find the boys sleeping peacefully and four bowls of the required color and size. In a rage, the lords split the mouths of the Whippoorwills leaving them as they are today.

HOW THE TWINS FAIR IN THE REMAINING HOUSES OF TERROR

The Xibalbans have now had enough of these two boys and so they confine them over the four days to the remaining four Houses of Terror. No more ball games, they just want to get them dead.

TEST #3 - COLD HOUSE

Here there are ice-cold drafts everywhere, thick-falling hail, icicles hanging from the roof, and sometimes even snow storms. They overcame the cold by huddling together wearing their ball game equipment the whole night and by just willing it to go away and get warmer. Which it did.

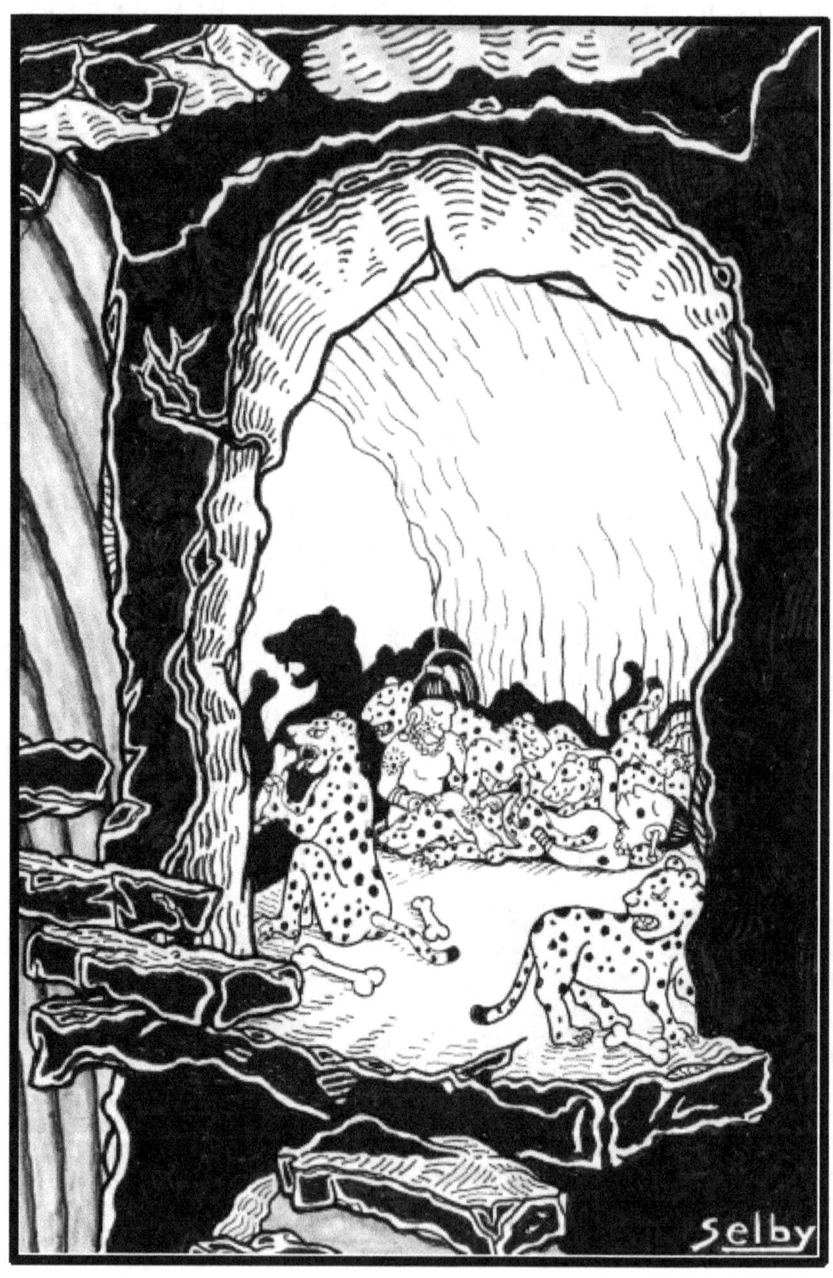
Selby

TEST #4 - JAGUAR HOUSE

TEST #4 - JAGUAR HOUSE

Full of hungry jaguars but the twins had grown up in the wild mountains and played with all of the animals in the wild. Xbalanque had always worn patches of Jaguar skin as a symbol of his respect for them. It helped that the boys had smuggled in bones of which there are many to be found in Xibalba. The jaguars were happy to growl and fight over the bones all night while the boys slept in a pile of warm jaguars.

In the morning the sentries went running with the news that the room was full of bones but their happiness was lost when the boys appeared ready for the next test

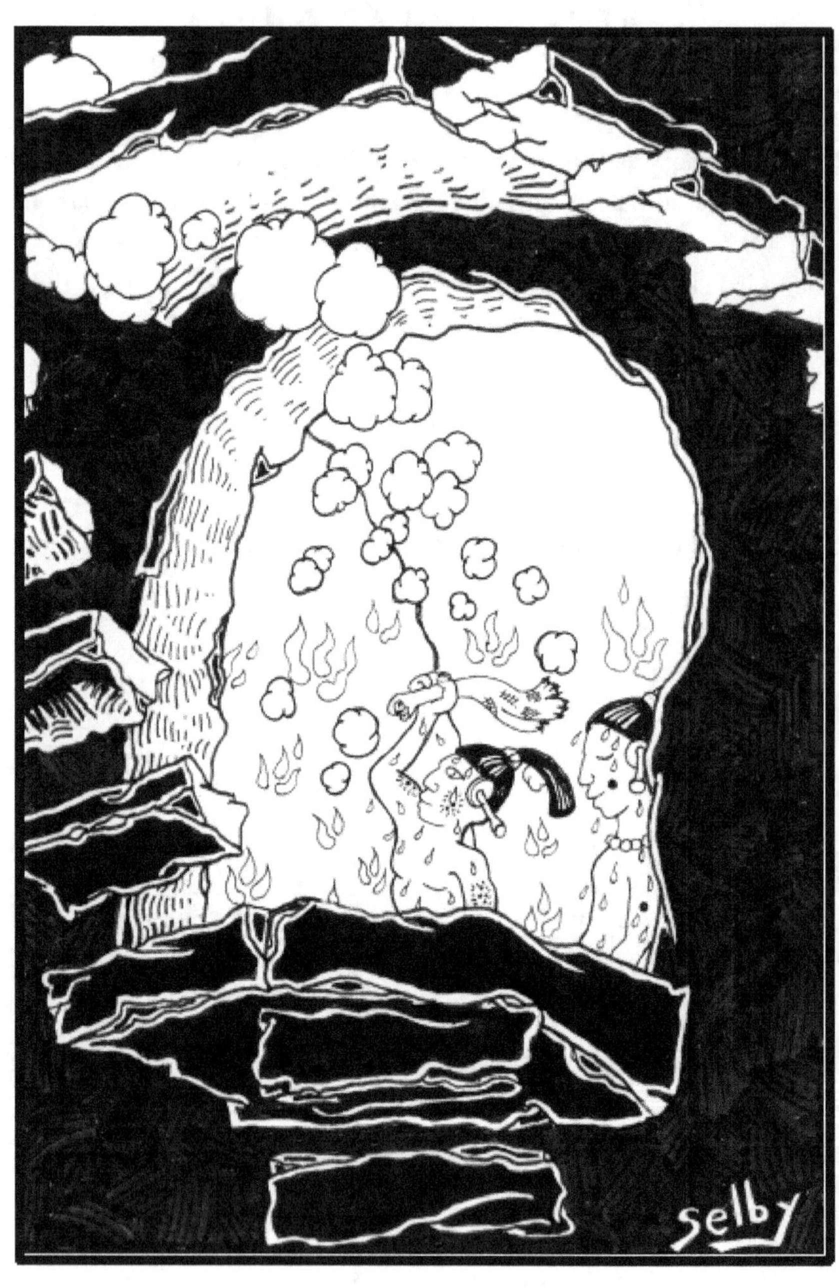

TEST #5 - HOUSE OF FIRE

TEST #5 - HOUSE OF FIRE

This was the most difficult for the twins. One of them must stay awake to stomp out or smoother the fires. They just took turns doing this or the fires would grow and engulf the whole room. They used a lot of their clothing pounding out the fires that broke out of holes and cracks in the walls and floor. It was probably very lucky for them that the fires only burned during the night.

Again the Xibalbans just couldn't understand who these two guys were. They began to think that these two could not die,

.

TEST #6 - BAT HOUSE

Next, Xbalanque and Hunahpu were pitted against the Snatch-bats. The Snatch-bats were monstrous beasts with snouts like knives, claws like thorns, and teeth like razors that screamed all night long.

The boys slept inside of their blowguns but didn't get much sleep. Sometime in the early morning things seemed to quiet down so Hunahpu thought it must be dawn and stuck his head out of the blowgun to take a quick look to see if it was morning, thinking that the bats had finally gone to sleep. Bad Idea!

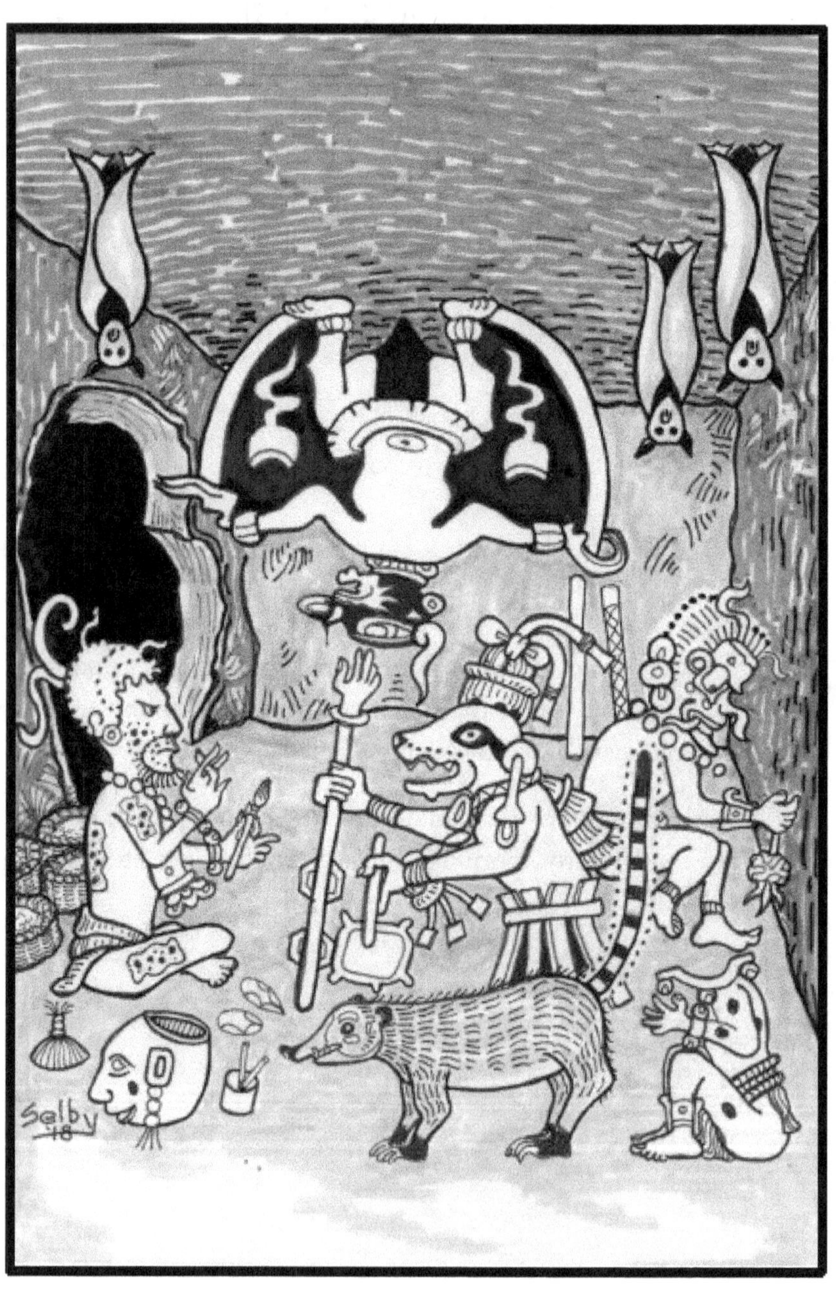

TEST #6, BAT HOUSE

His head was taken off by a snatch-bat leaving his body still stuffed in the blowgun. His head rolled out the door into the courtyard below where it was later used that morning to play ball.

Xbalanque couldn't come out of his blowgun because it was still night so he did the only thing he could in the situation and summoned Heart of Sky. Heart of Sky, who is as you remember called Hurakan, was brought forth by Possum who carried Hurakan in a chair on his back right into Bat House in the middle of Xibalba. Possum then went up into the sky and painted the red streaks of dawn so that the snatch-bats would go to sleep and the Xibalban would stay asleep. He had to do this many times to keep the day from coming.

Hurakan then summoned all the animals in Xibalba asking them to bring their food with them. The last to come was Coati who rolled a squash along the ground with his nose which is what they used to make a new head for Hunahpu.

Xbalanque then got busy carving a replacement head for Hunahpu. Hurakan had brought a small brain to replace Hunahpu"s. When Xbalanque finished the new head and placed it on Hunahpu's body Hunahpu could talk again. Everyone thought the head couldn't fool the lords of Xibalba for long so they made a plan. This plan included the help of the rabbit and the hope that Hunahpu's real head would be brought to the ballcourt by the Xibalbans.

They would just have to wait and see.

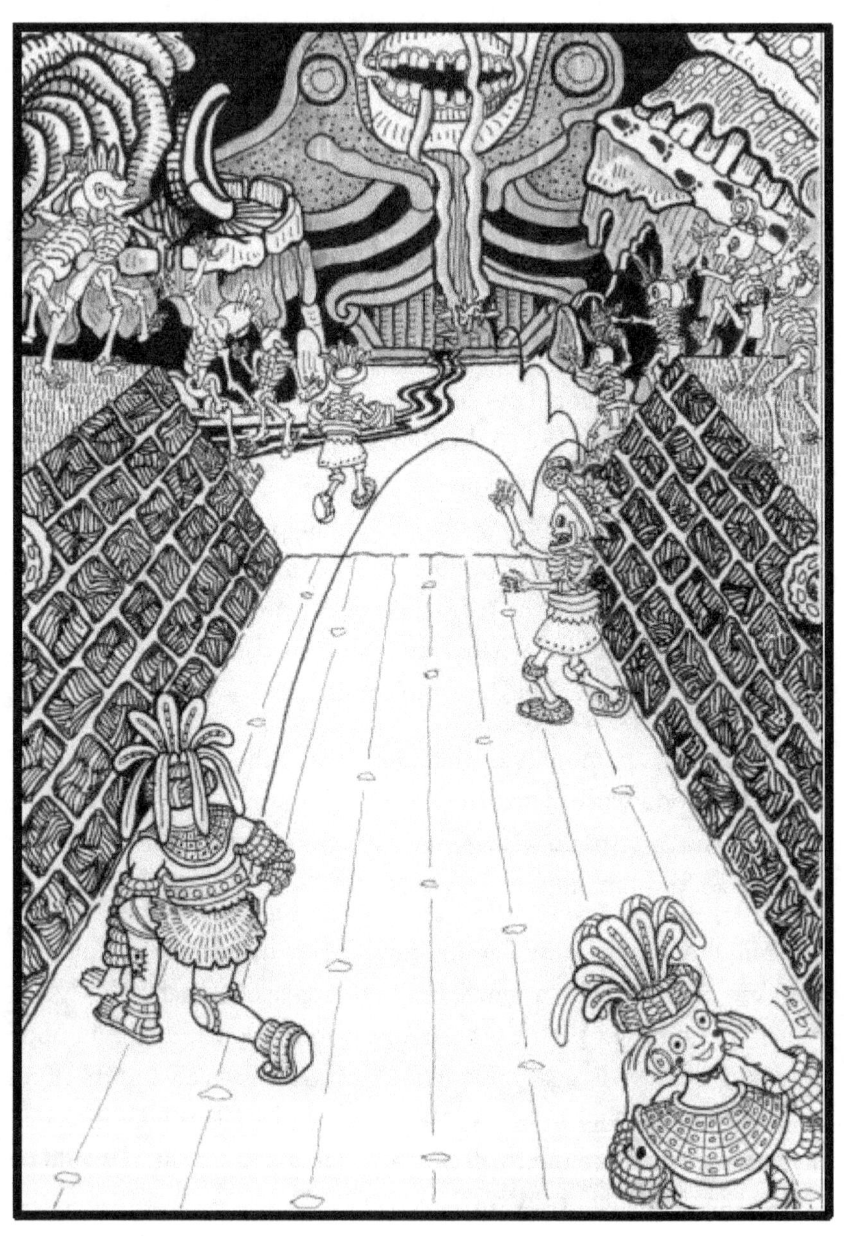

THE PLAN - CHASE THE RABBIT

THE PLAN - CHASE THE RABBIT

This plan called for the rabbit to hide himself in the ball bags. If the lords found the head of Hunahpu they would bring it with them and most likely would want to use it. Xbalanque would then hit the head into the ball bags and the rabbit would then run off and all of the Xibalban would go after the rabbit thinking it was the head or ball or whatever. This should give Xbalanque time to get Hunahpu's old head back in place.

Xbalanque instructions to Hunahpu were that he should not do much moving around until Xbalanque fixed his old head in place but he could shout at the Xibalbans as much as he liked.

When Xbalanque Hunahpu and the rabbit concealed in the ball bag arrived early the Xibalbans were already waiting for them.

"We have won! You're done! Give up! You lost," they shouted.

"On, no you haven't! We haven't even played ball yet! Just put that head in and let us get on with this stupid game," Hunahpu yielded at the top of his voice.

The lords of Xibalba were unable to explain what this head was that they had found in the courtyard that morning. So they had to put the ball (Hunahpu's real head) into the game. Xbalanque was on it in a flash and hit it so hard that it was well out of the ballcourt and in the ball bags before

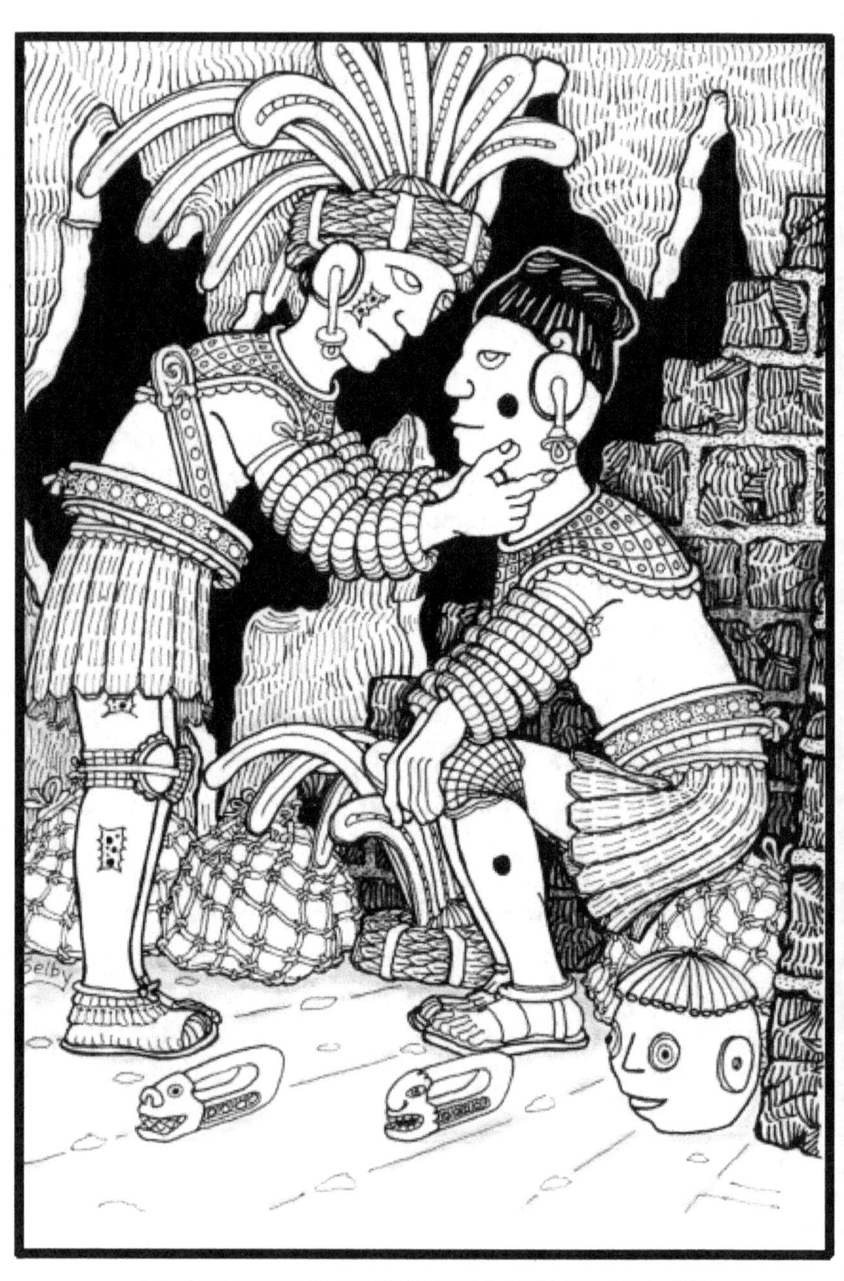

HUNAHPU GETS HIS HEAD BACK

anyone have time to think? The rabbit took off hopping with all of the Xibalbans, shouting and shrieking in pursuit.

HUNAHPU GETS HIS HEAD BACK

So the head of Hunahpu was a head again and with it back in place, they called the Xbalbans saying, "Come back! Here is the ball, we have it."

This ball looked just like Hunahpu's head because it was the head that Xbalanque had made for Hunahpu from the squash that Coati had brought. But, being just a squash it didn't last up to the hard play. When it split open that could have been the end of the twins but when the small brain that Hurakan brought fell out on the ballcourt floor and not a bunch of squash seeds the Xibalbans were once again tricked.

Now all of the Xibalbans have come together. Xbalanque and Hunahpu know that the Xibalbans are thinking of how to overcome them because they haven't died or been defeated by any of the tests or animals of Xibalba. In their hearts, they know that they must soon die and this death will be a fire, and that it must be of their choosing.

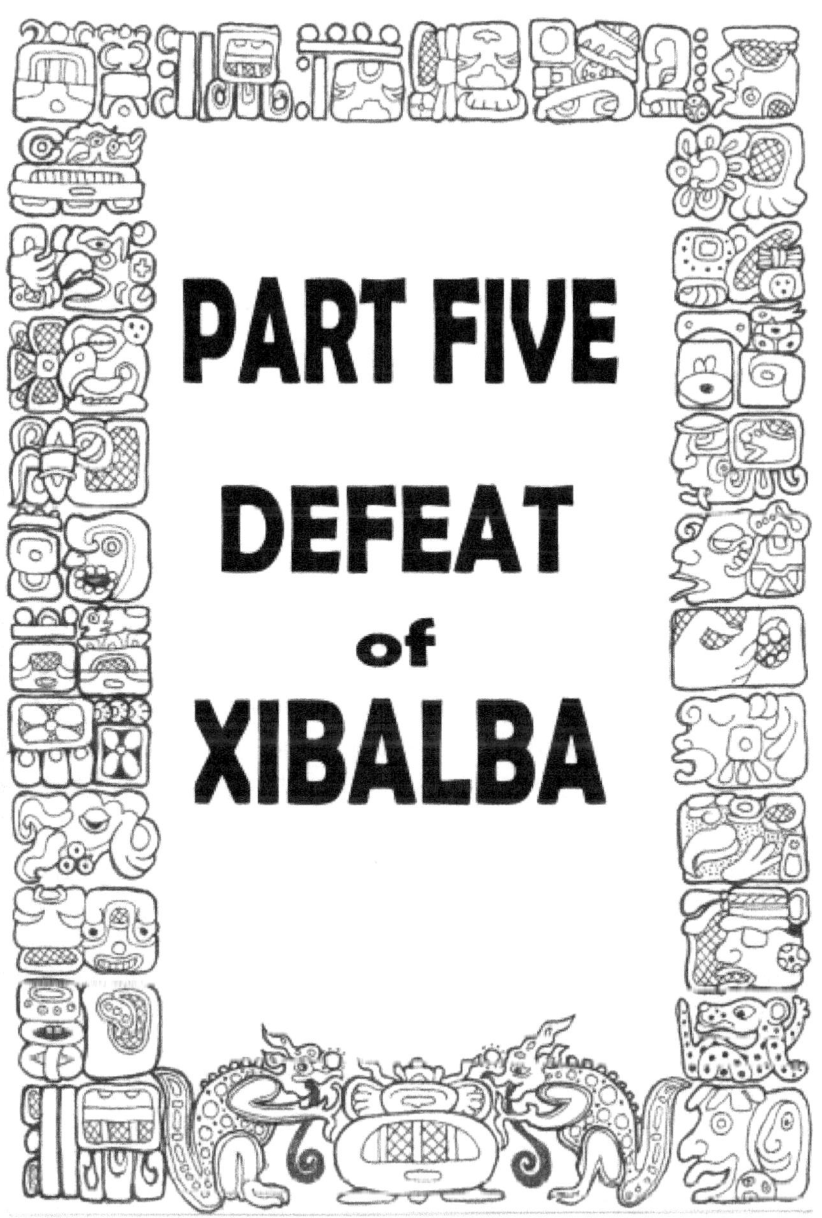

PART FIVE

THE FIRE

On the day of the making of the great fire for the oven that the Xibalbans used to make their sweet cacao drink, they made a larger fire than normal. It was so large that a person could fit in it, or actually, two people could fit in it.

When the fire was made up and fired the lords of Xibalba told their messenger owls to summon Xbalanque and Hunahpu to their new oven. "Just tell them that they must come! We have cooked up a treat for them."

In expectation of this moment, the twins had summoned two midmost seers. These were sent to earth by Hurakan as great knowers and were known as Xulu and Pacam.

Xbalanque and Hunahpu explained that there would be questions from the lords of Xibalba about our death. "We have not been defeated by anything that they have tried but soon the time will come when we must die. This death will be in their stone oven. So this is our plan;"

"If they ask you, 'Wouldn't it be good if we dumped their bones in a canyon?' "You should say, 'Hmm, it might not be good, since they would only come back to life again."

"If they say to you next, 'Then we will just hang them in a tree!' "Say, 'That is not good, since you will see their faces."

"Then they will speak to you a third time, 'Well, then, we will just throw their bones into the river." " Say, 'This is a good death for them, and it would also be good to grind their bones on a stone, just as hard corn is refined into flour, refine each of them separately."

"And, then add;

"Spill them into the river,

Sprinkle them on the waterway,

Among the mountains, small and great."

After receiving The twins' instructions, Xulu and Pacam set off for Xibalba to be available to the lords and set the twins' plan in motion.

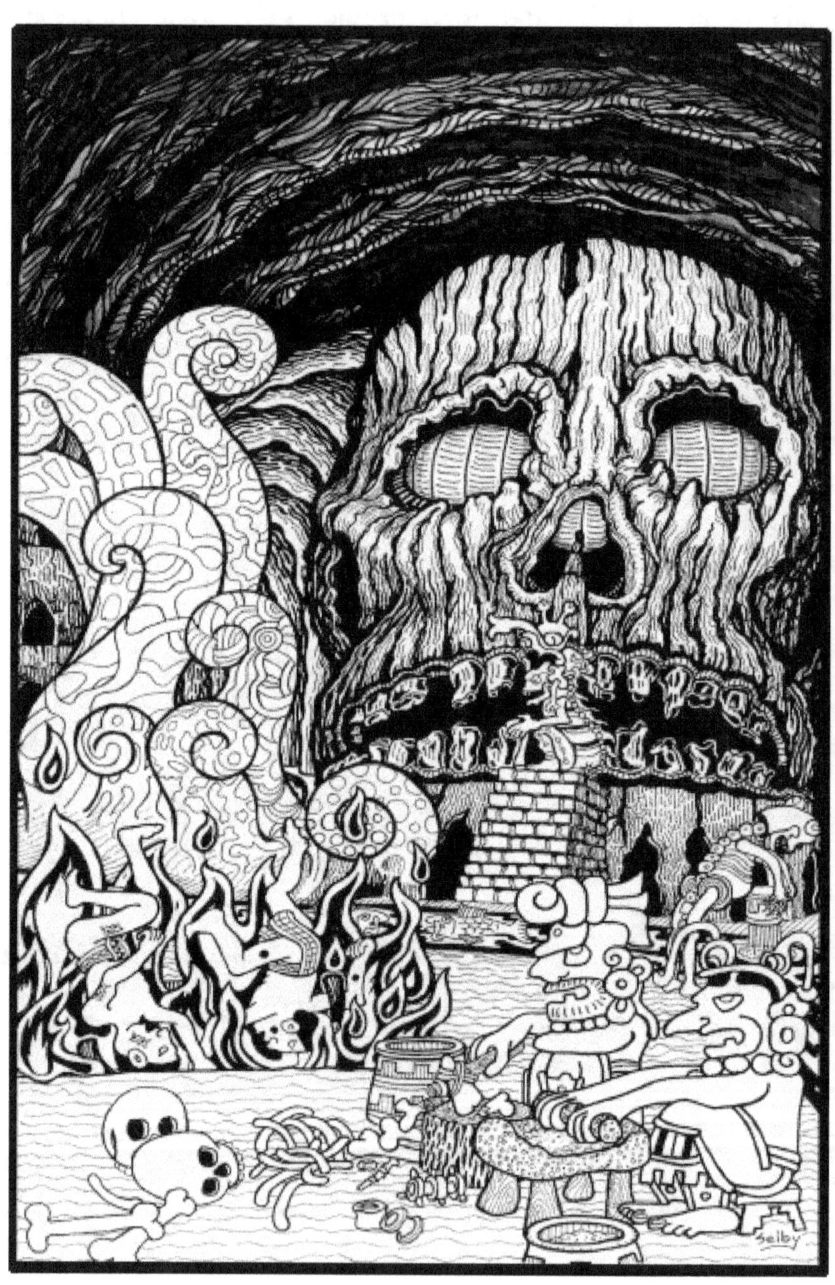

THE JUMP

THE JUMP

When the summons from Xibalba came, the twins quickly went to where the fire was prepared. Once there the lords wanted to play games like, "bet you can't jump over the fire blindfolded," but the twins were there for a reason.

"Don't you think we know what our death is, you lords?" the twins said, "Watch!" They grabbed each other by the hand and jumped head-first into the blazing fire. And there they died together in front of all the Xibalbans.

At first, there was complete silence except for the crackling of the fire. Then slowly the Xibalban started shouting and cheering. At last, they had triumphed over these guys. Or so they thought.

Xulu and Pacam kept their word and helped the lords decide what to do with the bones of the two boys. Their bones went where the twins wanted. Once they were ground and spilled in the river, they didn't go far. They just sank to the bottom of the river unnoticed.

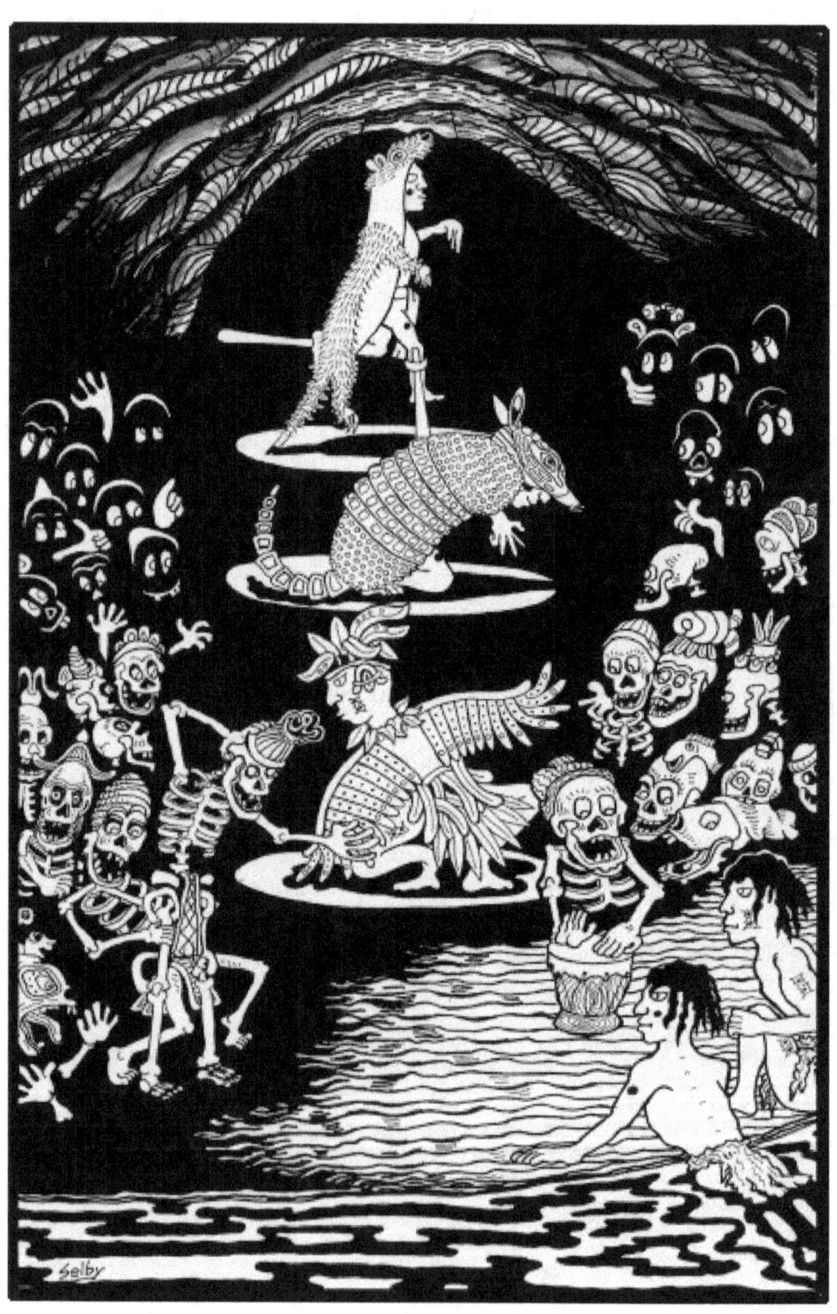

XBALANQUE AND HUNAHPU REAPPEAR

XBALANQUE AND HUNAHPU REAPPEAR

On the fifth day, they reappeared in the water where those who saw them said they looked like catfish. Having germinated in the water they appeared the following day as two vagabonds draped in rags. They looked the same as before, two very handsome boys but, they acted differently, they danced!

It was an uneasy sight for the Xibalbans to see the resurrection of the two boys who sprang from the water that their ground-up bones had been thrown in. And then to joyfully dancing with perfection dances only known to a few. The boys danced the Poorwill, the dance of the Weasel, and the dance of the Armadillos, to name but a few.

Not only was their dancing perfection, but they included swallowing swords and dancing on stilts creating costumes from thin air. They performed many miracles. Each out doing the next. They would set fire to a house and dance around it, then restore the house as it was.

As the intensity grew the twins began to sacrifice themselves, one of them dying for the other, right in front of everyone. The Xibalbans went crazy at the sight of their blood and their death and they would come back to life and begin a new more outrageous dance.

Everything that they did was the groundwork for their defeat of Xibalba. The pain, the agony, the destruction, and the cruelty were what made the Xibalbans so happy that they fell about laughing and crying and screaming in complete ecstasy.

ANOTHER SUMMONS BY THE LORDS

"Who are these vagabonds? Are they really so great? Is their dancing really that good? Can they do all of the things that are said of them?" the lords began to ask.

"We must see for ourselves," the lords told their owl messengers. But, when the owls gave their instructions to the boys they said, "They didn't want to go."

"Just plain NO!" they said. "We are afraid to go there, inside of such a lordly house. Take pity on us! Others have asked us to play today, so we can't do likewise for the lords, and likewise is not what we want," Said Xbalanque and Hunahpu.

The messengers made it clear that they had no choice in the matter and reluctantly they slowly made their way to the lords.

BEFORE THE LORDS

Feigning great humility, they bowed their heads to the floor when they arrived. They brought themselves low, doubled over, and flattened out on the ground. They looked the part of vagabonds when they arrived.

They were quizzed about where they came from and who were their parents but they maintained that they were orphans and did not know about their parents and they lived alone in the mountains.

"Well then," said the lords, "just entertain us. First, dance to sacrifice yourselves, then set fire to my house and after that, you will dance all of the things that you know. We want to be entertained. This is our heart's desire, this is the reason that you have been sent for." So they began their

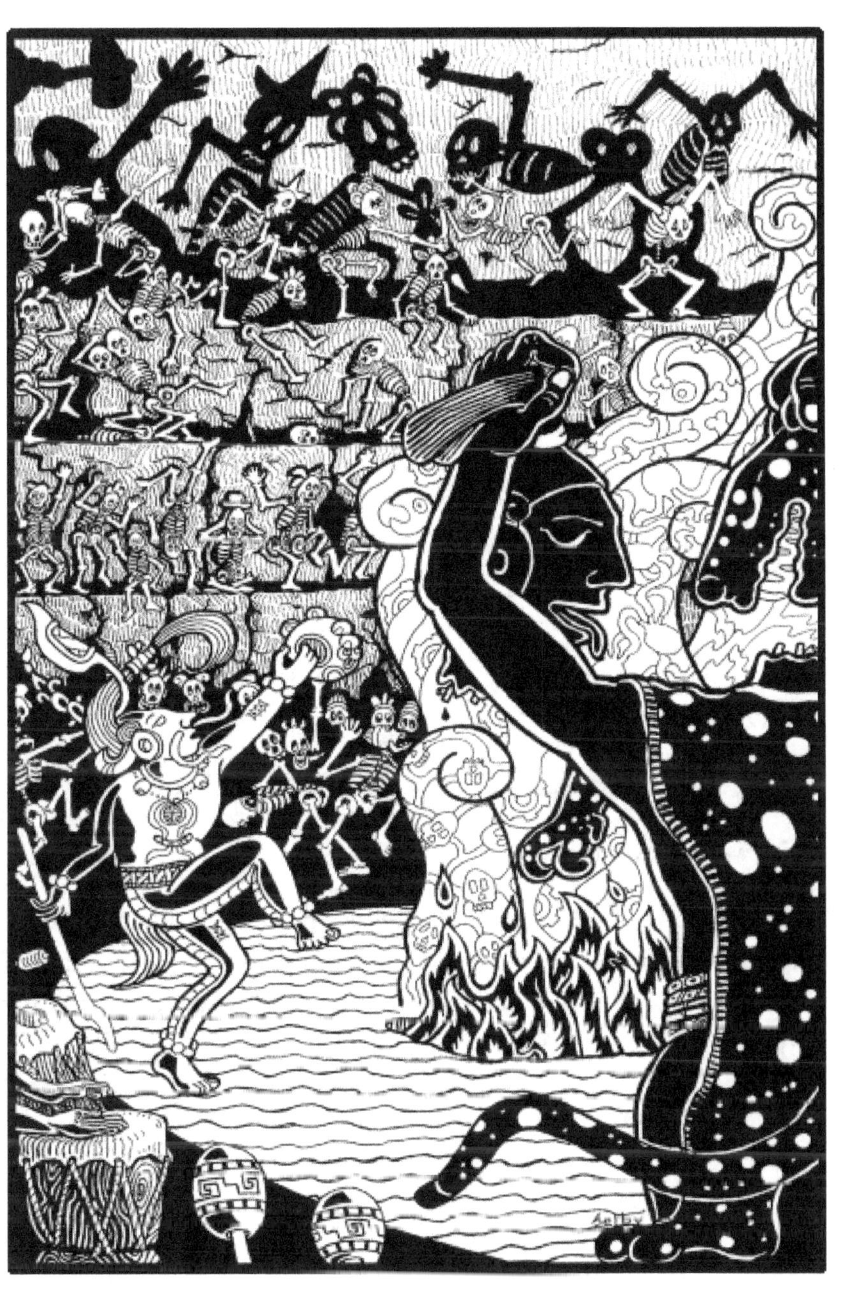

THING BEGAN TO GET OUT OF HAND

songs and dances while all of Xibalba came to watch, crowding the room with onlookers. They danced everything until one lord told them to, "Sacrifice my dog, but bring him back to life."

The dog was duly put to death and so happy when he was brought back to life that he ran around to everyone wagging his tail and kissing them on the cheek. A very happy dog that one.

As the crowd was worked up to a frenzy, they were told that they had not yet set the house on fire and then they did just that. The house was packed but no one was burned as panic raged with the fire. Everyone was overjoyed when they quickly put it out.

"You haven't killed anyone yet! Make a sacrifice without death," someone called out from the frenzied crowd.

THING BEGAN TO GET OUT OF HAND

"Very well," they said.

Then Hunahpu held a struggling body as Xbalanque held up a beating spurting heart for all to see. He then took it to One and Seven Death to admire then returned it quickly to the body that Hunahpu was holding and it came back to life screaming with joy.

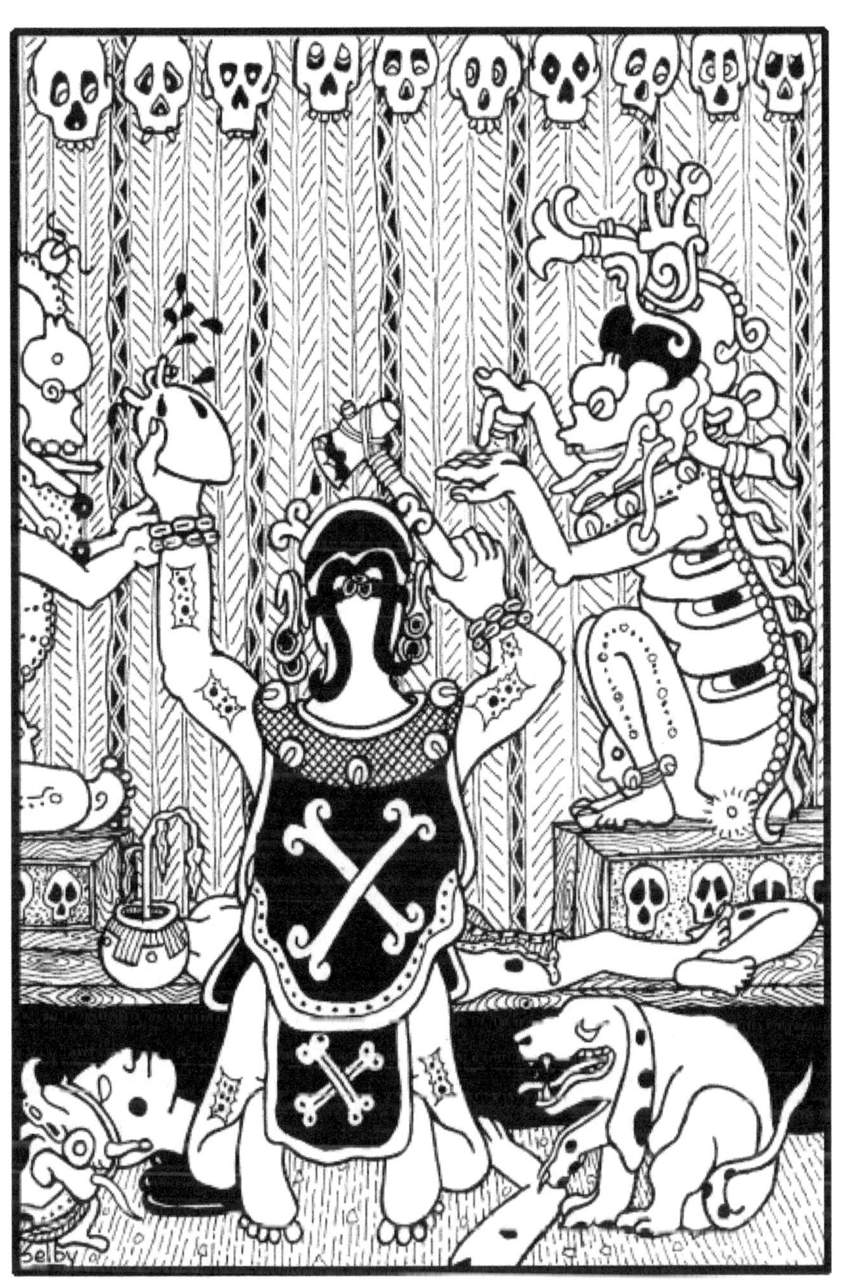

THE SACRIFICE OF LITTLE HUNAHPU

The lords and all of the Xibalban were amazed and close to hysterical at being in the presence of such

greatness. The crowd was swarming and jumping up and

down and started to chant, "Do it to yourselves, do it to yourselves."

THE SACRIFICE OF LITTLE HUNAHPU

Xbalanque and Hunahpu walked up to the platform where One and Seven Death sat. Hunahpu with a smile on his face, kneeled before the lords as Xbalanque raised his stone axe as the crowd roared.

One by one Xbalanque cut off the legs of this brother.

Then his arms.

Then his head came off.

Then his heart was cut out and held up high.

The Xibalban just went crazy at the sight, screaming, shouting, and throwing themselves about while only Xbalanque danced about the body of his brother.

When he suddenly stopped and shouted out, "Come on Hunahpu, let us dance together and suddenly Hunahpu was all together again and dancing wildly with everyone else. Needless to say both of the boys were very pleased at how it came out. Each amazed at himself at actually having done that awful "Dance of death."

Then over the screaming and madness came the clear words out of the mouths of One and Seven Death, "Do it to both of us!" Sacrifice us!"

THE DEFEAT OF THE RULERS OF XIBALBA

"Do it to both of us! Sacrifice both of us," said the rulers of Xibalba, One Death and Seven Death. Their hearts and whole being yearning for the "Dance of Death."

"Very well. You ought to come back to life. After all, what is death to you?"

And this one was the first to be sacrificed. The lord at the very top, One Death, is the ruler of Xibalba of the Underworld.

The second to be sacrificed was Seven Death. They were not brought back to life.

Such was the defeat of the rulers of Xibalba.

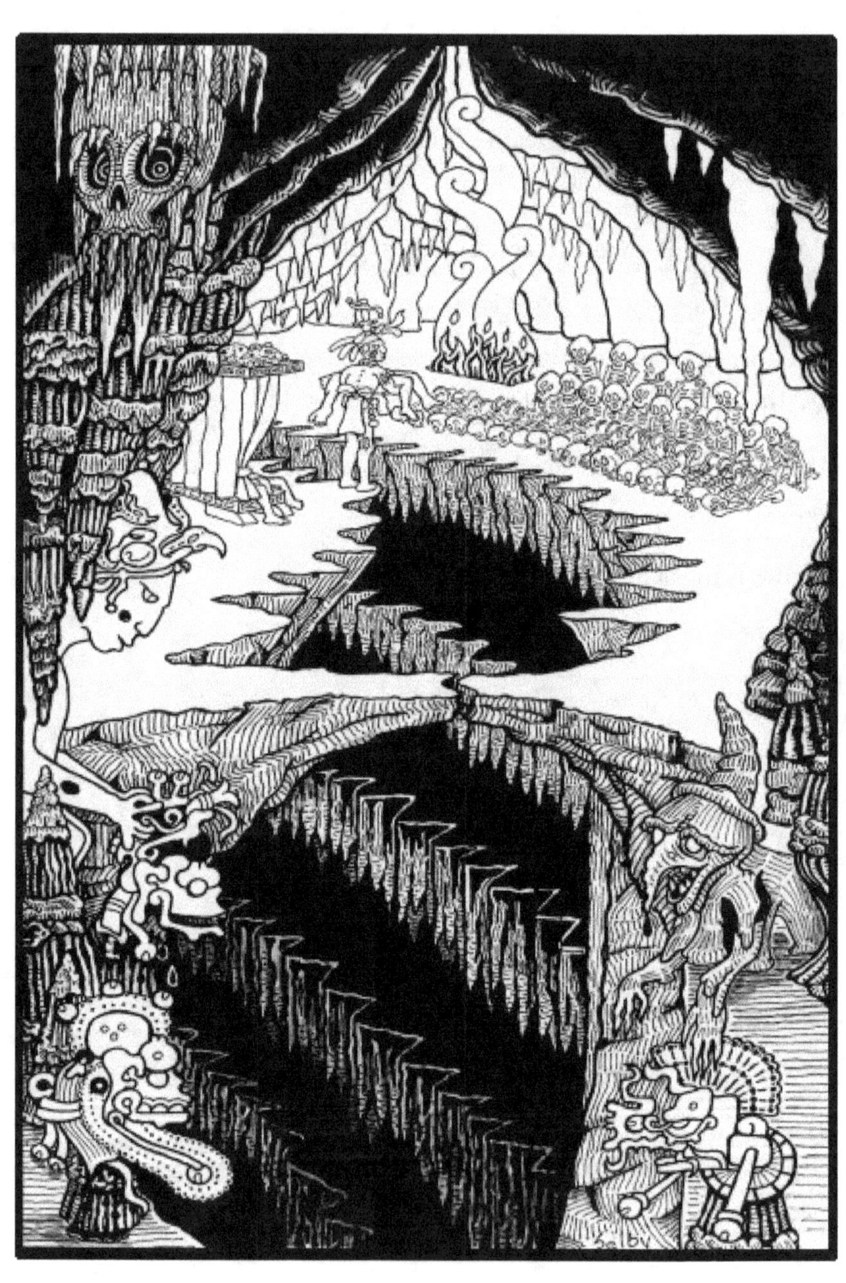

THE HERO TWINS SPEAK TO THE XIBALBANS

THE HERO TWINS SPEAK TO THE XIBALBANS

"Now this is our word. We shall name it for you. You will from this day forth only feed on the creatures of the meadows and clearings. None of those who are born in the light, begotten in the light will be yours. Only the worthless will yield themselves to you. These will be the guilty, the violent, the wretched, the afflicted. Wherever the blame is clear, that is where you will come in." said the hero twins of the Maya.

The Popol Vuh then tells us that these Xibalbans were an ancient race of people who only wanted conflict. They were the makers of enemies, users of owls, inciters to wrongs and violence, the masters of hidden intentions, masters of stupidity, masters of perplexity. Such was the loss of their greatness and brilliance.

This was accomplished by little Hunahpu and Xbalanque.

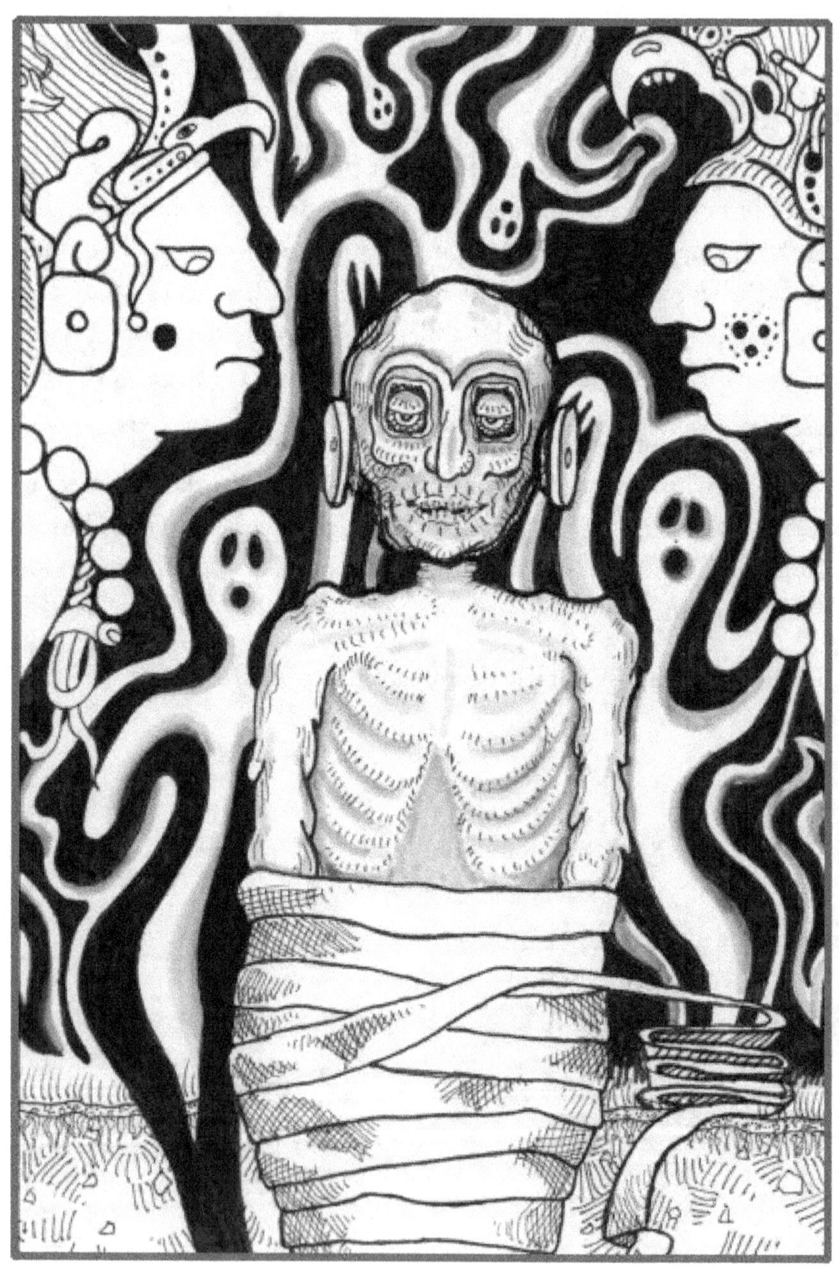

ONE HUNAHPU IS PUT BACK TOGETHER

ONE HUNAHPU IS PUT BACK TOGETHER

The hero twins went to the place of the Ball Game Sacrifice to put their father back together. He had wanted his face to become just as it was, but when he was asked to name the parts of his face he could remember, he named the mouth, the nose, and the eyes of his face but couldn't remember more. But, at least he had spoken again.

So it remained that they were respectful of their father, even though they left him there. Saying, "You will be prayed to here. You will be the first to have your day kept by those who will be born in the light. Your name will not be lost."

This in part did come true, for One Hunahpu became one of the most important gods of the Maya. He became the young and handsome "God of Corn," who is prayed to still in this age.

And here is where the two boys ascended to the sky where the Sun belongs to one and the Moon to the other and their story is still being told thousands of years later. And the Four Hundred Boys accompanied them to become the sky's stars while their mother Blood Moon looks over all of us each month as the goddess of the waxing moon.

THE GRANDMOTHER

The corn plants that the twins planted in the house of their grandmother had grown and then dried up. This was when they were burnt in the oven.

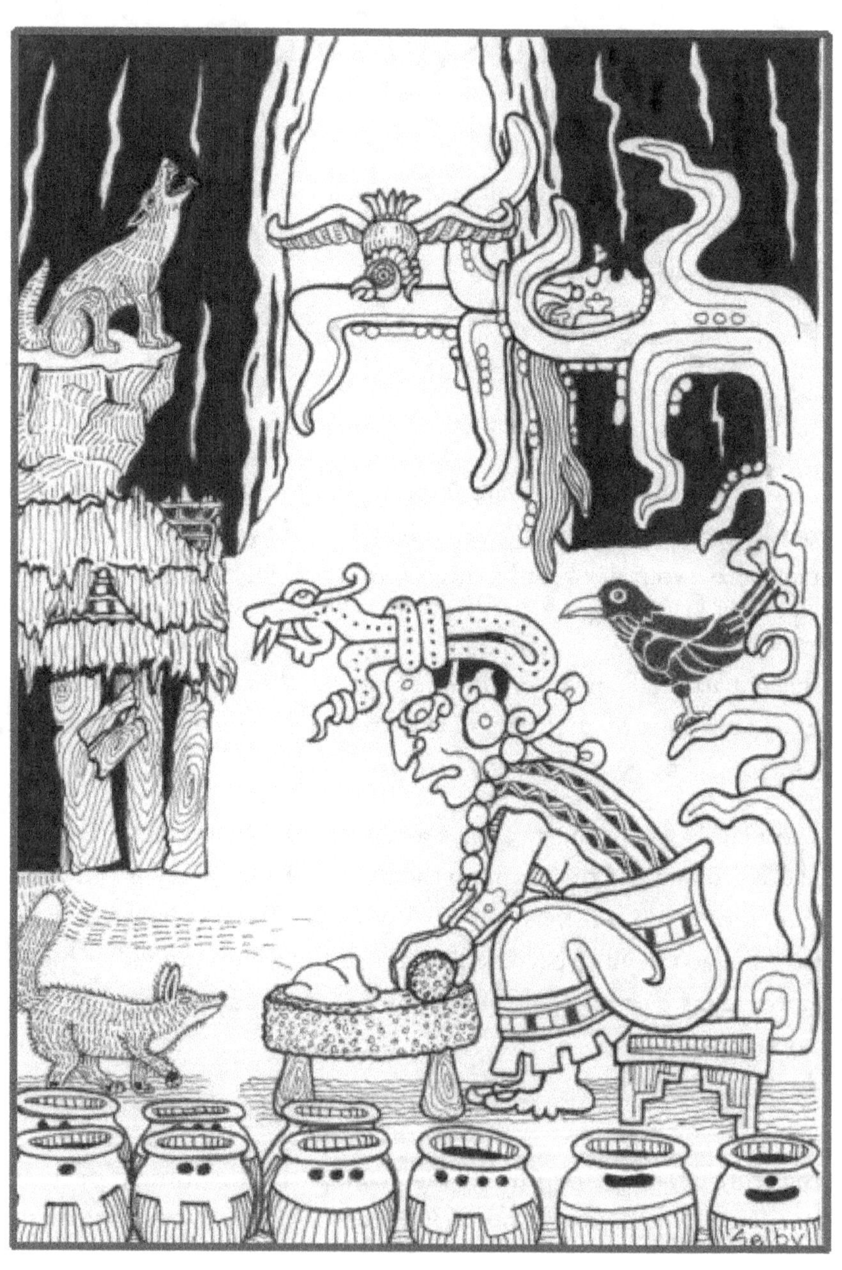

CREATION OF THE HUMAN WORKTHE 4th ATTEMPT

Then the plants grew again. This is when the grandmother burned copal before the ears of green corn as a memorial to

to them. There was happiness in the grandmother's heart the second time the corn plants sprouted.

CREATION OF THE HUMAN WORK

Heart of Earth and Heart of Sky had first created the animals in the hope that they would speak to their creator and be able to count days but this had not come to be. Then Xmucane and Xpiyacoc were brought to Earth to help but after two tries nothing further had been attempted.

At last, the long wait for the creation of Human Work had come. One day the animals named the Fox, Coyote, Parrot, and Crow brought a portion of food that they loved and had found in a mountain known as Split Place. This was yellow and white corn.

Sovereign Plumed Serpent and Hurakan thought this might be just what was needed for the flesh of the Human Work. Xmucane was given the task of preparing the yellow and white corn for the making of the first four humans. She ground the corn nine times to a super fine powder and she then made the grease for these first humans from the water that she rinsed her hands in.

Sovereign Plumed Serpent then modeled the first four humans. These were named:

The first person: Jaguar Quitze.

And now the second: Jaguar Night.

And now the third: Not Right Now.

And the fourth: Dark Jaguar.

These were the first people that were made and modeled. They came out human. They talked and made words. They looked and they listened. They walked and worked. They were good people.

Perfectly they saw and perfectly they knew everything under the sun. The Sovereign Plumed Serpent did not want this. He did not want a race of gods and at first thought, he would have to try yet again but, settled on taking back some of our understanding. So we are left with the ability to love, to learn, to understand what is right and what is wrong. Perhaps even a lot more.

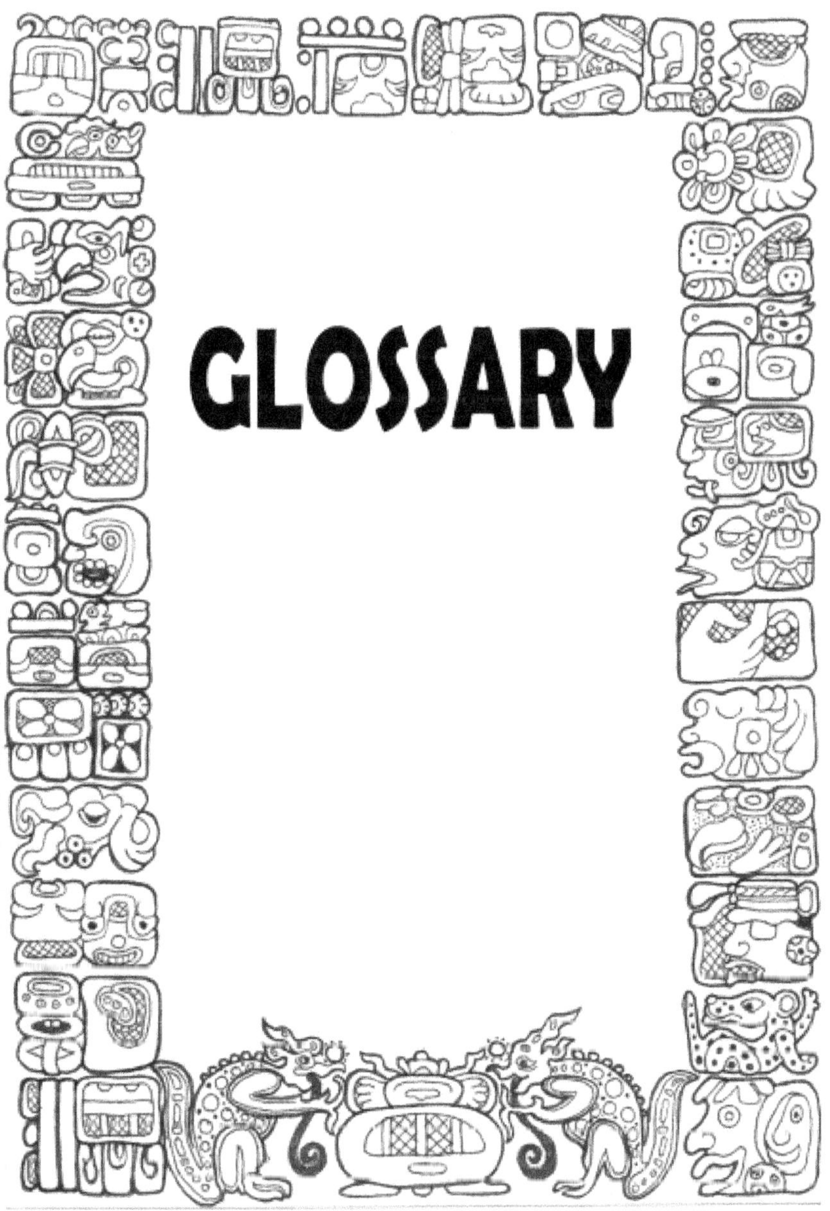

GLOSSARY

GLOSSARY

ARMADILLO (dance) - Name of a dance done by Xbalanque.

BALL COURT - A stone courtyard found throughout Mesoamerica typically with high stone walls that slanted outward at the top and contained a large stone with a hole for the ball to pass through usually located in the center of the wall near the top.

BAT HOUSE - One of six tests in Xibalba required of newcomers. Each was required to pass a night in one of these houses.

BEARER, BEGETTER - Names the PV gives for the gods who make the earth, the animals, and humans. These gods are also referred to as; Maker, Modeler. The gods are Sovereign Plumed Serpent and Hurakan.

BLACK ROAD - One of the four cosmic roads. On earth, the Black Road is the road to the west. On a cosmic plane, the Black Road is the Great Rift in the Milky Way which lies in Sagittarius. See Crossroads and Road to Xibalba.

BLOOD GATHER - Fourth-ranking lord of Xibalba. Said to collect human blood through violence or illness. In the PV he is the father of Blood Moon who will become the mother of the Hero Twins.

BLOOD MOON Daughter of Blood Gatherer and mother of Hunahpu and Xbalanque. In the Quiche version of the PV, she is said to be the goddess of the waxing moon while her mother-in-law, Xmucane, is the goddess of the waning moon and her son Xbalanque becomes the god of the full moon. However, other Mayan sources indicate that Saq Ixiq was the goddess of the moon. Like so many other intriguing problems in Maya cosmology perhaps one day we will know more.

BLOOD RIVER - A river that crosses the road to Xibalba.

BLOODY TEETH, BLOODY CLAWS - Two lords of Xibalba.

The eleventh and twelfth ranking lords. Here is another confusion since the PV has two lists of the Underworld lords. On the first list these two lords appear and on the second list Demon of Filth and Demon of Woe appear in the same place. It may be that these are the same lords under different names.

BONE SCEPTER, SKULL SCEPTER - Seventh and eighth-ranked lords of Xibalba.

BROMELIADS - Air plants (Tillandsia spp.) A prevalent type of plant that colonizes in high places such as trees. Some variates look like the tops of pineapples and have a stiff center stock. These were used by Hunahpu and Xbalanque in constructing the arms and claws of a fake crab to bring about the demise of Zipacna.

CACO WOMAN, and CORNMEAL WOMAN - The goddesses whom Blood Moon calls forth to help her collect corn. They are also known as Thunder Women and Yellow Women.

CALABASH - The fruit of a lowland tree (Crescentia Cujete). The fruit when dried forms a very hard shell that was used for cacao beverages. In Xibalba, the tree in which One Hunahpu's head was placed had not borne fruit until this event.

CHIMALMAT - (shield net) Wife of Seven Macaw and mother of Zipacna and Earthquake. Common to the Popol Vuh, names often refer to objects, calendar dates or cosmic objects. In the case of Seven Macaw, the stars of the Big Dipper, while hers form a circle that includes the arc of the Little Dipper.

COATI - A raccoon-like omnivorous, tree-dwelling mammal (Nasua narica). It has a long snout and a long ringed tail that it holds erect. It is found from Arizona to South America in mostly lowland forest areas.

COLD HOUSE, RATTLING HOUSE - One of the tests of Xibalba where one must pass the night in freezing conditions. This may correspond to a position in the Mayan zodiac.

COPAL - A type of incense found throughout Mesoamerica made from the resin of the Incense Tree (Bursera bipinnata).

COUNCIL BOOK - Popol Vuh or popo vuj, the hieroglyphic book used by the council of Quiche lords to see into the past or future.

CROSSROADS - a four-way intersection of the roads that link the cosmos together. At the celestial level, this is where the ecliptic crosses the great rift of the Milky Way near Sagittarius. In the PV it is where the Road to Xibalba meets the Black Road, Green Road, Red Road, White Road, and Yellow Road.

CROTON - "Red tree" or "cochineal red tree", called "Sangre de dragon" in Spanish (Croton sanguiferous). The sap of this tree is red and suggests blood when it flows fresh from the tree. In the PV a large nodule of this sap is used to trick the lords of Xibalba into thinking it is the heart of Blood Moon.

DARK HOUSE - Another test in Xibalba where one must spend the night in total darkness. This may have reference to a position on the Mayan zodiac.

DAWN OF LIFE, THE - A descriptive phrase for the Popol Vuh referring to the first dawning of the present sun. Also, "Our Place in the Shadows" or "The Life in the Light" would be alternative readings.

DAYKEEPER - Diviners who count the days of the divinatory calendar using Cora seeds. The daykeepers in the Popol Vuh are Xpiyacoc and Xmucane.

DEMON OF FILTH, DEMON OF WOE - The ninth and tenth in earlier lists but are omitted from later ones. See Bloody Teeth, Bloody Claws.

EARTHQUAKE - Name of the second son of Seven Macaw and Chimalmat; younger brother of Zipacna, He loses his great strength in his limbs when he eats a bird coated with earth and ends up buried in the earth. His continuing attempts to move cause the earthquakes we feel.

EGRET WOMAN - Wife of One Hunahpu and the mother of One Monkey and One Artisan. Her name comes partly from the Yucatec name for the snowy egret (Egretta thula).

FALCON - A messenger for Heart of Sky. (see laughing falcon).

FOUR HUNDRED BOYS - The group of young boys who try to kill Zipacna but are killed by him instead. They become the stars of the Pleiades and other stars. They were the makers of alcoholic drinks.

GRANDMOTHER OF DAY, GRANDMOTHER OF LIGHT - Phrases used for Xpiyacoc and Xmucane meaning grandmother for as long as day or light have existed or may exist.

GREAT WHITE PECCARY, GREAT WHITE COATI - Refers to the white-lipped peccary (Tayasu pecare), a small wild pig, and the coatimundi (Nasua narica) a relative of the raccoon. The names of the old couple that Hunahpu and Xbalanque call forth who tell Seven Macaw they deal with problems of bones and teeth.

HEART OF SKY, HEART OF SEA - Refer to the gods otherwise called Hurakan, Newborn Thunderbolt, and Sudden Thunderbolt.

HEART OF LAKE, HEART OF SEA - The gods are known as makers, modelers, and as Bearer, Begetter and they include Sovereign Plumed Serpent. They cooperate with the Heart of Sky, and Heart of Earth to create the features of the earth and the animals and plants.

HUNAHPU - (Junajpu) Known sometimes as "Little Hunahpu." He was foremost a hunter and ballplayer and the elder twin brother of Xbalanque. He is usually referred to first when their activities occur on the earth's surface. Their mother was Blood Moon whose father was the fourth lord of Xibalba. Their father was One Hunahpu (and perhaps jointly his twin Seven Hunahpu). The astronomical roles of Hunahpu include that of the planet Venus, which still bears his name when it appears as the morning star, and that of the sun that appeared on the first day of the present age. Hunahpu is also the name of one of the volcanoes made by Zipacna.

"HUNAHPU MONKEY" - Title of a tune played on the flute by Hunahpu and Xbalanque. One Monkey and One Artisan, having been turned into monkeys came to the edge of the forest when called by this tune.

HUNAHPU POSSUM, HUNAHPU COYOTE - May refer to Hunahpu and Xbalanque in their role as vagabond dancers and magicians whose arrival signals the transition of one solar year to the next.

HURAKAN - (Hurricane, Tohil) He is known as Thunderbolt Hurricane and Heart of Sky, Heart of Earth, Tohil, he was a first-ranking patron deity of the Quiche people in one of his earthly forms. He is also the god who evoked the rain and flood that carried away the wooden people and who gave instructions to the Hero Twins.

JAGUAR HOUSE - One of the tests of Xibalba. Maybe a position on the Mayan zodiac.

LAUGHING FALCON - A snake-hunting falcon (Herpetotheres cachinnans) that was seen over ball courts. It received its identifying black eye patch from a bit of rubber from the ball of Hunahpu and Xbalanque.

THE LIGHT THAT CAME FROM BESIDE OF THE SEA - Another name for the Popol Vuh.

MACAW OWL - The third-ranking Military Keeper of the Mat for the Principal Bird Deity of Classic Maya vase paintings, who has the head and wings of a horned owl but the tail of a macaw.

MAKER, MODELER - Names given to the gods who gave form to the earth, plants, animals, and humans. These gods are also called Bearer, and Begetter and they include Sovereign Plumed Serpent.

MATCHMAKER - (Mamon) One who arranges marriages and conductor of marriage ceremonies. Xpiyacoc was such a person.

MIDMOST SEERS - Diviners who can foresee the future. This term was applied to Xpiyacoc and Xmucane, One and Seven Hunahpu, Xulu, and Pacam in the PV.

NETTLES HEIGHTS - (Chuwi la) The town known nowadays by its Nahus name, Chichicastenango, which means "Nettles Citadel." Formally a Cakchiquel citadel but today the inhabitants speak Quiche. Also, the area is where the Quiche Popol Vuh was written.

NEWBORN THUNDERBOLT, SUDDEN THUNDERBOLT - Gods whose names refer both to shafts of lightning and to fulgurites (glassy stones formed where lightning strikes sandy soil, conceived as projectiles hurled from the sky). These same gods are the Heart of

Sky, and Heart of Earth, with Thunderbolt Hurricane they form a threesome.

ONE DEATH, SEVEN DEATH - The first and second-ranked lords of Xibalba, named after two days on the divinatory calendar. In the PV they are treated as two different persons, but one and seven stand for all thirteen possible numbers occurring first and last among the number prefixes of any given day name. By putting the severed head of One Hunahpu in a tree, they initiate evening-star appearances of the planet Venus that begin on days named Death.

ONE HUNAHPU, SEVEN HUNAHPU - The elder and younger twin sons of Xpiyacoc and Xmucane, named after two days on the divinatory calendar. In the PV they are treated as two persons, but one and seven stand for all thirteen possible numbers occurring first and last among the number prefixes of any given day name. One Hunahpu is the father, by Egret Woman of the twins One Monkey and One Artisan. One and Seven Hunahpu are seen in the PV as jointly being the fathers, by Blood Moon, of the twins named Hunahpu and Xbalanque. By bringing the face of the dead One Hunahpu back to life, the twins initiate morning-star appearances of the planet Venus that begin on days named Hunahpu. One Hunahpu will become the maize god, his sacrifice by decapitation symbolized the taking of sweet ears of maize and he is the archetype of Mayan perfection and male beauty

ONE-LEGGED OWL - Second-ranking Military keeper of the Mat for the lords of Xibalba. One of four messenger owls. Owls only stand on one leg at a time.

ONE MONKEY, ONE ARTISAN - They are the sons of One Hunahpu and Egret Woman. They are half-brothers to Hunahpu and Xbalanque. They are the patron deities of musicians, writers, and artisans. One Monkey (a howler monkey) is named for the corresponding day on the Kekchi and Yucatec calendars.

PLACE OF BALL GAME SACRIFICE - The place where the decapitated body of One Hunahpu and the complete body of Seven Hunahpu were buried by the lords of Xibalba. Probably not a place name, but rather a name for the altar where losing ballplayers were sacrificed.

POORWILL, DANCE OF THE - A dance done by Hunahpu and Xbalanque in Xibalba.

POPOL VUH - See Council Book.

PUS RIVER - A river that crosses the road to Xibalba.

QUETZAL - Also known as Resplendent Quetzal (Pharomachrus mocinno) Found only in cloud forest habitats scattered from Chiapas to Panama. It is the most spectacular bird in the New World. Bright green with blue iridescence with red breast and white accent under the tail. With two-foot-long tail feathers, it was a major item of tribute and a major feature of lordly regalia throughout Mesoamerica.

QUICHE - (K'iche) The name of a subgroup of the Maya nation centered in the highlands of Guatemala.

RATTLING HOUSE - One of the tests of Xibalba. Also known as Cold House.

RAZOR HOUSE - One of the tests of Xibalba was stone knives whirling about the room all night.

ROAD TO XIBALBA - This is the road that One and Seven Hunahpu followed down into the Underworld known as Xibalba. This road had several obstacles or tests and after the Crossroads, they took the Black Road. The Quiche PV places this road in or near a place they called, "Great Hollow with Fish in the Ashes." As a celestial road, it is the Great Rift in the Milky Way.

RUSTLING CANYON, GURGLING CANYON - This was on the Road to Xibalba. It may be east of San Pedro Carcha in Guatemala where the Rio Cahabon disappears into a system of caves and then emerges again.

SCORPION RAPIDS - This was another feature on the Road to Xibalba. It may correspond on a celestial level to where the ecliptic crosses the Great Rift in the Milky Way. This would be located in Scorpius which the Maya also saw as a scorpion.

SEVEN MACAW - A very interesting and controversial figure. Some scholars see him as a pre-Mayan god who had been replaced in Mayan cosmology and was symbolically killed by Hunahpu and Xbalanque in the PV. The PV sees him as a god who falsely claimed to be both the sun and moon during the era of the Wooden people (the people before the Maya). Seven Macaw is the husband of Chimalmat and the father of Zipacna and Earthquake. In his earthly role, he is Scarlet Macaw, while his celestial role is the seven stars of the Big Dipper. Hurakan has Hunahpu and Xbalanque brings Seven Macaw down from his tree opening the way for the great rain that destroys the wooden people who worshipped Seven Macaw as the sun. (Note: the great rain is thought to be the great flood that affected the whole world. This escapade in the PV may reflect that traumatic event).

SHOOTING OWL - First-ranking Military keeper of the Mat for the lords of Xibalba, one of the four messenger owls.

SKULL OF ONE HUNAHPU - Refers to the calabash fruit which is said to have never occurred until the head of One Hunahpu was placed in the tree in Xibalba.

SKULL OWL - Forth-ranking Military Keeper of the Mat for the lords of Xibalba, one of the four messenger owls.

SOVEREIGN PLUMED SERPENT - The principal deity who helped create the features of the earth and the animals, plants, and humans. The Plumed Serpent features more in early Mexican civilizations than in the Maya. It has been suggested that at the time of the writing of the Quiche PV, there was significant pressure by the Spanish clergy not to refer to traditional gods. One of many things not fully understood.

SPLIT PLACE, BITTER WATER PLACE - The place where the Makers and Modelers got the corn and water needed to make the bodies of the first true humans. Xmucane ground the corn that was found there by the Fox, Coyote, Parrot, and Crow.

SWALLOWING SWORDS - A dance where two performers in masks shake tortoiseshell rattles, pound themselves on their chests with stones, and put sticks down their throats and bones up their noses. Hunahpu and Xbalanque perform this dance after they are reincarnated in Xibalba.

SWEET DRINK - (Ki') An alcoholic beverage made from maguey, known in Mexico by its Nahuatl-derived name, pulque. Ki' can mean not only "sweet' but "poison" as well.

THRONG BIRDS - A migrating flock of Swainson's hawks (Buteo swainsonii) which migrate through Guatemala in large numbers.

THUNDER WOMEN, YELLOW WOMEN - The protective goddess that guards the crops of One Monkey and One Artisan's garden. Also known as Cacao Women and Cornmeal Woman. Toj and Q'anil are day names from the divinatory calendar that are days for harvesting ripened ears of corn which is what Blood Moon is doing when she asks the help of these guardians.

WALKING ON STILTS - A dance done by Hunahpu and Xbalanque.

WEASEL, DANCE OF THE - A dance performed by Hunahpu and Xbalanque.

WHITE DAGGER - Refers to a sacrificial stone knife belonging to the lords of Xibalba. During the first ball game, there were several hidden in the ball.

WHITE ROAD - One of the four cosmic roads. White is the color of the north on Earth, but the White Road of the sky is the section of the Milky Way that is solid white.

WING AND BACKSTRAP - Lords of Xibalba who rank eleventh and twelfth in the list of lords and ninth and tenth in the later list. A backstrap is a piece of hide used to protect the forehead when a load is carried with a tumpline.

XBALANQUE - (Xb'alang'e) A hunter and ballplayer, the younger twin brother of Hunahpu. Their mother was Blood Moon and their fathers were One and Seven Hunahpu. Both are referred to as the Hero Twins. In the PV Xbalanque was the dominant twin while they were in the Underworld. The astronomical roles of Xbalanque include the night or underworld sun and the full moon. His name means "sun's hidden aspect" in Kekchi (a Quichean language).

XIBALBA - (Xib'alb'a) The Underworld beneath the surface of the earth, ruled by One Death and Seven Death with other lords. The Sun passes through the Underworld when it is not in the sky.

XPIYACOC, XMUCANE - Divine grandparents, older than all the other gods. Parents of One and Seven Hunahpu and patrons of daykeepers. To this day the ideal daykeepers are husband and wife and the divinations with the clearest outcomes are the ones they do together. They are also midwives and matchmakers, which are specialized subfields of contemporary Quiche diviners. In the PV they are referred to as Grandmother of Day, Grandmother of Night (though Xpiyacoc is male) Bearer twice over, and Begetter twice over (as if to make them even older than the gods who are simply called Bearer, Begetter).

XULU, PACAM - Diviners who tell the lords of Xibalba to throw the ground bones of the Hero Twins into a river with the result that they become catfish and then themselves.

ZAQUICAZ - The snake that swallows the toad that swallows the louse that carries the message from Xmucane. It is a thick, black snake that is said to flee when it sees people, making a noise with its belly.

ZIPACNA - The first son of Seven Macaw and Chimalmat and the elder brother of Earthquake. He claims to be the maker of the earth and has the character of a caiman. Like most Mayan gods he has a human form as well as an animal form.

Don't miss out!

Visit the website below and you can sign up to receive emails whenever Steven Selby publishes a new book. There's no charge and no obligation.

https://books2read.com/r/B-A-SWXDB-PRXYC

BOOKS 2 READ

Connecting independent readers to independent writers.

Did you love *The Popol Vhu*? Then you should read *Money, Money, Money, The 1%*[1] by Steven Selby!

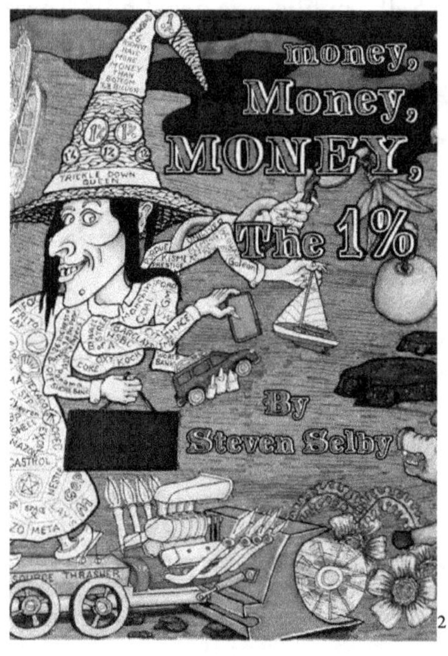

If a picture is worth 1,000 words and seemingly money is the most pressing thing in life, while poetry stimulates the mind's passions, then they all join hands to look at the extreme imbalance of wealth affecting society today. Based on a central pen and ink, the mural is broken down into components and stitched together with poetry. The imaginary setting is a pandemic of the One Percent of the US population that has accumulated half of the world's wealth and explores this on different levels. While the author supports the need for change, he focuses on leaving the readers free to make their own choices by casting their votes in democratic elections. While the mural is set in the United States, it applies to much of the world's political policy. He also encourages

1. https://books2read.com/u/m0a0j0

2. https://books2read.com/u/m0a0j0

further debate on a more equitable model for the preservation of resources and the suitability of human presence on Earth.

For many years the author was an Architectural draftsman and found greater pleasure in drawing friends and the many different things he encountered while traveling. Rather than following the trend of computer-generated drawing in architecture, he dedicated his time to creating wooden sculptures and developed his unique organic architecture using all manner of natural materials. Recently he has also written a book titled, "The Stories from the POPOL VUH" featuring 50 of his charming illustrations with the stories arranged for all reader levels. This ability to use the simple materials of pen and ink has influenced his work in political dialogue and he has ambitions to use these skills for further political statements.

The 'Money, Money, MONEY', is a cartoon mural that is a light-hearted romp across the US political landscape with many comments and poems in which the author hopes to influence us to work together to protect our physical world and create more equality. The reader will find the original drawing with about 30 detailed illustrations of characters of the 1% representing BIG TECH to Big Meat and APEZON to THE TRAMP with layers of poems and comments.

Also by Steven Selby

Money, Money, Money, The 1%
The Popol Vhu

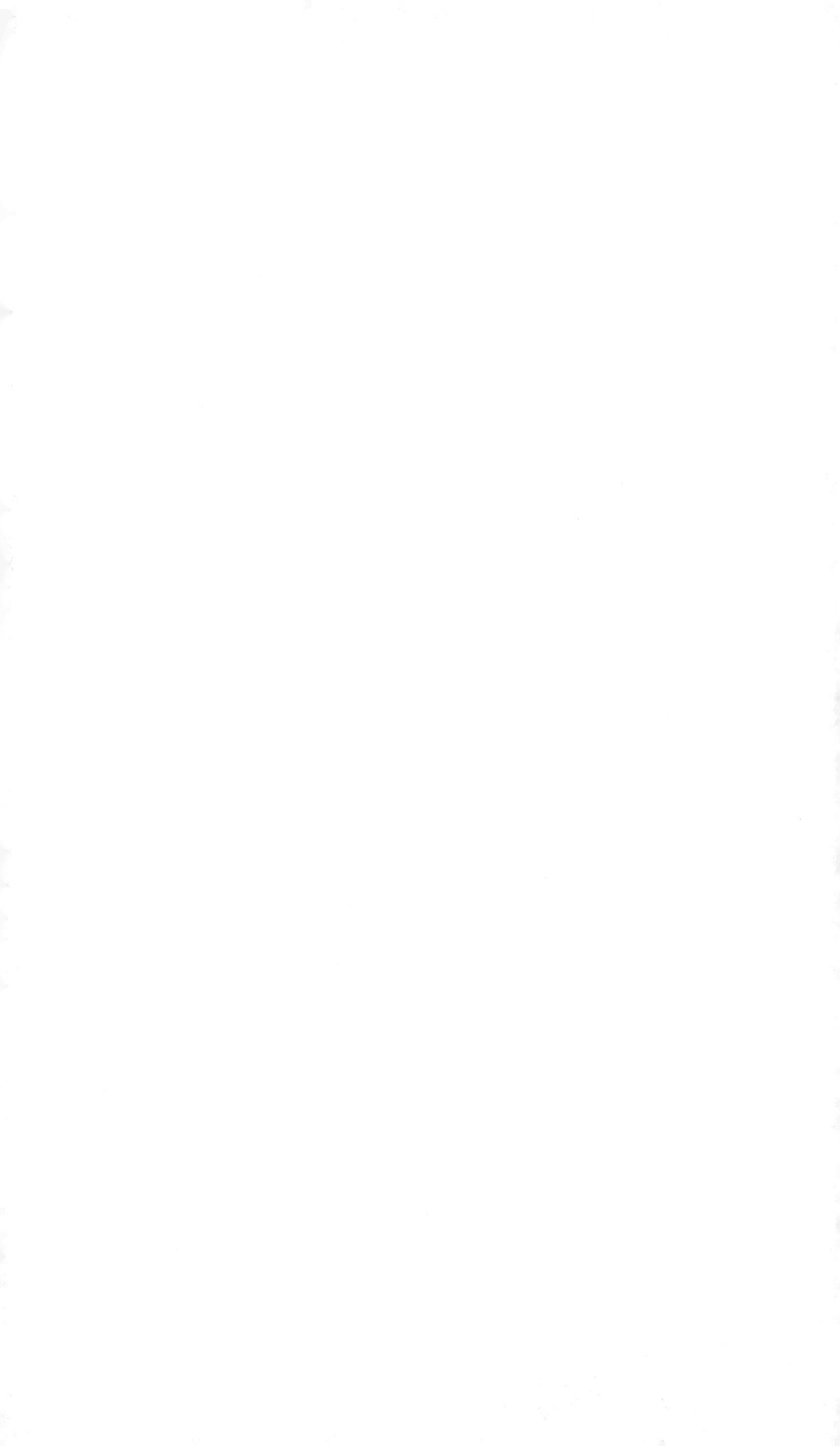